IN THE REALM OF THE LAST MAN

ALSO BY FRANCIS FUKUYAMA

Liberalism and Its Discontents

Identity: The Demand for Dignity and the Politics of Resentment

Political Order and Political Decay

The Origins of Political Order

America at the Crossroads: Democracy, Power, and the Neoconservative Legacy

State-Building: Governance and World Order in the 21st Century

Our Posthuman Future

The Great Disruption: Human Nature and the Reconstitution of Social Order

Trust: The Social Virtues and the Creation of Prosperity

The End of History and the Last Man

IN THE REALM OF THE LAST MAN

FRANCIS FUKUYAMA

First published in Great Britain in 2026 by
Profile Books Ltd
29 Cloth Fair
London
EC1A 7JQ
www.profilebooks.com

First published in the United States of American in 2026 by Farrar, Straus and Giroux

Designed by Patrice Sheridan

Photograph of Covid ward on page 162 by Hao Ke.
All other photographs are courtesy of the author.

Ornament on title page, dedication page,
and chapter openers by 100ker/Shutterstock

1 3 5 7 9 10 8 6 4 2

Printed and bound in Great Britain by
CPI Group (UK) Ltd, Croydon CRO 4YY

A CIP catalogue record for this book is available from the British Library.

Our product safety representative in the EU is BGC Sustainability & Compliance, 7 avenue du Général Leclerc, Paris, 75014, France https://baldwinglobalconsulting.com

Hardback ISBN 978 1 80522 771 7
Trade Paperback ISBN 978 1 80522 799 1
eISBN 978 1 80522 773 1

TO MY GRANDCHILDREN,
THOSE ALREADY BORN
AND THOSE YET TO COME

CONTENTS

PREFACE

ON JANUARY 20, 2025, DONALD J. TRUMP WAS SWORN IN as the forty-seventh president of the United States. His second term marked a major shift in global politics.

The United States is the world's oldest and best-established liberal democracy. While the country has had a checkered past of deviations from the ideal set forth in the Declaration of Independence that "all men are created equal," it has over 250 years created a remarkable space for liberty and prosperity in North America. More than that, since 1945 it has labored to create a liberal world order, where other liberal democracies could flourish and interact.

The second Trump administration has broken from these traditions, both at home and abroad. Domestically, Trump has ruled through a cascade of executive orders, bypassing Congress and issuing diktats that appeared on their face unconstitutional, illegal, or reflective of extremely bad judgment. Internationally, he has sided with the world's dictatorships, such as Russia, at the expense of fellow liberal democracies.

And he has at a stroke dismantled the liberal economic order by imposing arbitrary tariffs on friendly countries under the claim that America was being exploited by the open economic world it itself had created.

All of this comes against the backdrop of declining democracy and rising authoritarianism around the world. Beginning in the early 1970s, the world experienced what Samuel Huntington labeled the "Third Wave" of democratization. The number of democracies around the world rose from somewhere in the thirties to well over a hundred in subsequent decades, as Communism fell and authoritarian opponents such as Russia and China liberalized their systems. But beginning at around the time of the global financial crisis of 2008, the Third Wave went into reverse, and has been receding ever since. This was the product of big authoritarian countries such as Russia and China consolidating their rule and seeking to project their influence beyond their borders. One of the greatest expansions of human freedom occurred between the fall of the Berlin Wall in 1989 and the dissolution of the Soviet Union in 1991, but in 2008 Putin's Russia began a project to restore the Soviet domain. This included invasions of Georgia in 2008 and Ukraine in 2014.

This period from 2008 on also saw the rise of populist nationalist leaders in a number of important countries, including Turkey, India, Hungary, Brazil, and elsewhere. The most important of these populists was Donald Trump, whose initial election in 2016 signaled a global shift away from the liberal principles around which the earlier order had been built. Several months into his second presidency, it is hard not to recognize that he is trying to turn the United States into an authoritarian country.

In addition, there are a number of voices on both the extreme right and left that have been openly criticizing the basic ideas underlying the liberal order, beginning with politicians such as Hungary's Viktor Orbán, who claims to be building an "illiberal democracy" in his country. On the left, many young people think of themselves as socialists, as opposed to liberals or social democrats.

So we are very clearly in a different historical period than the one that existed in the late 1980s. My essay "The End of History?," published in the summer of 1989, and the book version, *The End of History and the Last Man*, published in 1992, have been taken to be expressions of naive liberal triumphalism, and I have been asked several times a week over the past three decades whether I wished to recant my argument. I have written thousands of words and given dozens of interviews seeking to answer this question.

None of the individuals asking have read more than the title of my essay or book. In particular, none bothered to read the last five chapters of my book, which dealt with the problem of the Last Man. Those chapters explored the different ways in which liberal democracy might break down in the future, and suggested that History, rather than ending, had simply paused on its way to an uncertain future.

The very title "The End of History?" was borrowed from the great Russian-French interpreter of Hegel, Alexandre Kojève. Kojève saw the historical process as being driven less by a contest over material resources than by a "struggle for recognition," in which human beings sought to have their fundamental dignity acknowledged. For most of human history, this led to an unequal contest between masters and slaves, until the advent of the French Revolution, which established the principle of equal recognition as the only rational solution to the human problem. This was the basis for the liberal order that stemmed from that revolution, a principle that subsequently spread through much of the world.

The problem, though, is that the peace and prosperity brought about by a liberal order based on equal recognition is not enough for many people. They do not want to be recognized as the equals of every other person on earth; they want to be recognized as superior in some respect. Liberal societies focus their members on the narrow pursuit of peace and prosperity, and have been good at delivering on that promise. But the being who emerges at the end of history is typically someone stripped of struggle, risk, and ambition, someone whom the philosopher Nietzsche labeled the "Last Man."

We have been living in the realm of the Last Man for some time now. The extremism that we see on both the right and the left is in some sense a revolt against the flattened horizons created by liberal societies, in which we are enjoined to be endlessly open and tolerant and nonjudgmental. There is of course material deprivation and injustice in the liberal world today. But populist anger is driven much more by resentment against a society that does not distribute respect equally, and that anger drives a push to use political power to right the balance. That anger does not envision an alternative set of institutions that will correct these perceived wrongs; it simply wants to tear down as much of the existing order as possible.

It is perhaps worth quoting the last paragraph of my original essay:

> The end of history will be a very sad time. The struggle for recognition, the willingness to risk one's life for a

purely abstract goal, the worldwide ideological struggle that called forth daring, courage, imagination, and idealism, will be replaced by economic calculation, the endless solving of technical problems, environmental concerns, and the satisfaction of sophisticated consumer demands. In the post-historical period there will be neither art nor philosophy, just the perpetual caretaking of the museum of human history. I can feel in myself, and see in others around me, a powerful nostalgia for the time when history existed. Such nostalgia, in fact, will continue to fuel competition and conflict even in the post-historical world for some time to come. Even though I recognize its inevitability, I have the most ambivalent feelings for the civilization that has been created in Europe since 1945, with its north Atlantic and Asian offshoots. Perhaps this very prospect of centuries of boredom at the end of history will serve to get history started once again.

IN THE REALM OF THE LAST MAN

1

MY CALIFORNIA DREAM

I ARRIVED IN CALIFORNIA FOR THE FIRST TIME AS AN adult in the summer of 1978, when I got a summer internship at the Rand Corporation in Santa Monica. Rand was the original think tank, created by the US Air Force in 1948 to study issues of nuclear strategy, an agenda that broadened subsequently to cover many other areas of public policy. I had driven all the way from State College, Pennsylvania, in the old Opel Kadett my parents had given me to my Aunt Fumiko's house on North Stanley Avenue in West Hollywood. I had failed to properly reseat the rocker cover gasket on the car's engine before I left; it started leaking oil somewhere in Arkansas and had to be towed to a garage. But it was clear sailing after that. I was following the old Route 66 (now Interstate 40): Oklahoma City, Amarillo, Gallup, New Mexico, Flagstaff, Arizona, Winona, Kingman, Barstow, San Bernardino, and then into the Los Angeles basin.

Aunt Fumi was one of the kindest and most open people I have ever met, and even after I moved to Santa Monica a few years later I spent a lot of time at her house with my four cousins on my father's side, Jack, Joe, John, and James.

Southern California from the first moment seemed like a magical place. In my years living in the East, I had never seen a city with so many Porsches and Ferraris, where infrastructure looked new, unlike the dirty, broken-down rights-of-way you see when you take the Amtrak from Boston to New York. Early on I found myself on Wilshire Boulevard driving behind a convertible Mercedes with the license plate RICHBICH, driven by a big-haired blond in a crop top the likes of whom I had never once encountered during my years in Cambridge, Massachusetts.

That summer I wrote a research report on Iraq's relationship with the Soviet Union, following on the dissertation I was completing on Soviet foreign policy in the Middle East. The senior analysts at Rand liked the study a lot, and it was one reason why they gave me a job offer at the end of the summer. Little did I know that Iraq would involve me in some big foreign policy controversies in the 1990s and 2000s.

After that summer, Rand asked me to work on a CIA contract to analyze some now-forgotten topic in Soviet Middle East policy. In contrast to the Pentagon, CIA clearances require polygraph tests, and I failed mine. If you have never been polygraphed, you may not know how stressful these tests can be. They asked me whether I had ever lied, which if you are an honest person is impossible to answer, as well as some embarrassing questions such as whether I had ever had sex with a man (the answer was no, but I suspect my heart rate shot up on hearing the question). I was planning at that point to work in the government, and I was terrified that if I failed to get an Agency clearance I would never be able to work at State or Defense. I must say, Rand was very supportive and hired a high-powered lawyer specializing in security issues, who forced the Agency to keep giving me tests until I finally passed one.

I returned to Rand as a regular employee in 1982, after my first stint on Ronald Reagan's State Department's Policy Planning Staff. Cheap housing was very difficult to find in the People's Republic of Santa Monica due to its strict rent-control laws; you had to know someone with a rent-controlled apartment to have any hope of finding an affordable place to live. On arriving, I saw an offer on the bulletin board at Rand for a room in a shared apartment posted by one of the secretaries. She was a rather attractive brunette somewhere in her mid-forties with a deep tan and freckles, who had a rent-controlled house close by in downtown Santa Monica. Having been told to come over lunch break, I showed up with my suitcase and found the front door open with no one apparently at home. I walked inside and wandered around; there were stairs leading up to a roof patio, where I found, amidst a jungle of marijuana plants, the secretary lying out on a chaise longue, completely naked. She told me to take the bedroom between her daughter's and that of her own seventeen-year-old boyfriend. He was the same age as her daughter, and had his own room in case they weren't getting along that day. When I met him in the evening, he turned out to be a bare-chested, suntanned surfer of California legend.

That was when I realized I wasn't in Kansas anymore, and certainly not in Cambridge, Massachusetts.

At the beginning of the 1980s, everyone I knew was divorced, or in the process of getting divorced. This was true of almost all of my new colleagues at Rand. We were in this period at perhaps the high point of what I later called "the Great Disruption," when changes in the nature of work altered the social norms governing the structure of the traditional nuclear family as well as many other social patterns.

To this young, single male in his late twenties, California thus seemed rather like a land of unlimited possibilities, sexual and otherwise. It was not, however, one that I was able to take much advantage of. Or at least, not to the extent that my Bulgarian colleague Alex Alexiev did. Like me, he worked on Soviet projects at Rand. I went hiking and skiing with him and his fellow Bulgarian friend Simon in the Sierra Nevadas, and admired his ability to attract women. Alex hated Communism, and would later return to Bulgaria to launch a political career after Bulgaria transitioned to elections in the early 1990s.

Since that time, I have regarded the Sierras as the most beautiful mountains anywhere in the Lower 48. My love for them was directly connected to my interest in photography, and I saw them—Mount Tom, Mount Whitney and the Alabama Hills, Tenaya Lake, the Minarets—through the eyes of Ansel Adams. He'd lugged an eight-by-ten wooden view camera up to the High Sierra with his pack animals, and waited for the perfect moment at dawn or in the middle of winter to snap his shutter, the lens stopped down to f/64 so that everything would be in sharp focus from six inches to infinity. The Range of Light made me appreciate why environmentalism had become so deeply rooted in the state, though that environmental consciousness would end up becoming a big liability by fostering an antigrowth mindset among activists.

2

"THE HOUSE WAS BEING FILLED WITH STRANGE INDIANS"

I HAVE BEEN LIVING IN NORTHERN CALIFORNIA SINCE 2010, and lived in Southern California for most of the 1980s. Though I was born in Chicago and grew up in New York City, I feel a much stronger attachment to California than to any other part of the country. In my humble opinion, there is nothing beautiful in the United States east of the Rocky Mountains. There are many dysfunctional things about the way California is governed today, but as many people have said, California is not just a beautiful physical environment but also a special state of mind.

Joan Didion's essay collection *Slouching Towards Bethlehem* has become a celebrated classic about the 1960s. The eponymous essay talks about the burgeoning hippie movement and Berkeley antiwar protestors. But my favorite piece in that collection is a short essay entitled "On Self-Respect."

In the essay Didion talks about what it means to have

"character"; that is, a sense of one's own worth that is not dependent on the opinions of those immediately around you. She argues—perhaps somewhat dubiously—that people in the nineteenth century had stronger character than her contemporaries, and then relates the following story about a pioneer family traveling west:

> It did not seem unjust that the way to free land in California involved death and difficulty and dirt. In a diary kept during the winter of 1846, an emigrating twelve-year-old named Narcissa Cornwall noted coolly: "Father was busy reading and did not notice that the house was being filled with strange Indians until Mother spoke about it." Even lacking any clue as to what Mother said, one can scarcely fail to be impressed by the entire incident: the father reading, the Indians filing in, the mother choosing the words that would not alarm, the child duly recording the event and noting further that those particular Indians were not, "fortunately for us," hostile.

I don't think you need to go back to the 1840s to find people with strong character and an internal sense of self-worth who could endure grave hardships on their way to California. There were at least two such women on my father's side of my family, my grandmother Shizu and my Aunt Fumiko.

My grandmother, born Shizu Yokota, was a "picture bride." My grandfather, Keikichi Fukuyama, had emigrated to the United States sometime after 1905 (the date is a little hazy, but family legend had it that he was escaping impressment into the Imperial Japanese Army for service in the Russo-Japanese

War). Shizu left Japan in 1920, taking a steamer to Los Angeles all alone, where she was to marry a stranger ten years older than herself. She was only twenty-one years old; there is a photo of her on the voyage where she looks very small and afraid. Her family was Christian, and she was married soon after her arrival in the States at the First Methodist Church in Los Angeles. She went on to have four children: twin boys, Hiroo and my father, Yoshio; and two girls, Fumiko and Kiku.

It turned out that my grandmother had many talents that only appeared in later years. She could play piano and the Japanese koto, and later turned to painting beautiful watercolors. She started her own dressmaking business on the second floor of her husband's hardware store at 307 East First Street in Little Tokyo, where she made dozens of dresses she designed herself for a local department store. Perhaps her greatest talent was as a writer, however. She kept a journal, and wrote a long series of letters to my Uncle Hiroo in the time they were separated during the Second World War. On Christmas Day 1942 she wrote:

> Christmas dinner was wonderful for a camp life. After dinner, we had a wonderful Christmas celebration . . . All the children up to fifteen years old received their Christmas gifts. I heard that these gifts were sent to us by many outside people who were sympathetic toward our children.

So even in the immediate aftermath of Pearl Harbor, there were kind Americans trying to help those mistreated by their own government.

My paternal grandfather, Keikichi; paternal grandmother, Shizu; Aunt Kiku; father, Yoshio; Uncle Hiroo; Aunt Fumiko

The other strong woman was my Aunt Fumiko. After the Japanese attack on Pearl Harbor, my father's family were sent to internment camps. This happened to all Japanese Americans on the West Coast, regardless of whether they were US citizens, in a policy upheld by the Supreme Court in its 1944 decision *Korematsu v. United States.* Keikichi and Shizu were sent to a camp in Amache, Colorado, while Fumiko, still a teenager, was assigned to another camp in Jerome, Arkansas. Some of the bitterness of that internment was expressed by my Uncle Hiroo in a letter to one of his teachers at LA City College:

> When our family evacuated, we had several unpleasant situations . . . My sister's ouster from the Civil Service and the losing of our store. We had several thousand

> dollars tied up in our store, and after we turned over our store to the Board of Trade, we found ourselves penniless . . . No matter what you may think when you enjoy the riches of freedom, once you lose that freedom there is a great psychological change that comes over you. No matter what people say about us not being held in a concentration camp, you have your freedom to do as other people curtailed; wait half an hour every mealtime in line to eat . . . whether you be a phi beta kappa, PhD, college grad you do any menial job given you; after they give an okay to being certain things they confiscate it . . . gosh this is democratic.

My father and my Aunt Kiku managed to avoid camp by getting scholarships to Doane College in Crete, Nebraska, just outside of Lincoln. I will be eternally grateful to these small liberal arts colleges that reached out to help Japanese American internees in this period, and would make similar gestures to Arab Americans after September 11. Decades later Doane College invited both my father and eventually me to speak at their commencement.

The Supreme Court eventually overturned *Korematsu v. United States*, and Ronald Reagan apologized to the Japanese Americans sent to camp, with Congress paying restitution to each of them. The first generation issei such as my grandparents took their treatment stoically; it was their children who had been Americanized into an understanding of their fundamental rights who led the redress movement in later years. Unfortunately, the wrong for which Reagan apologized was not truly internalized, and in 2025 the US government returned to mistreating people—this time, those suspected of being undocumented migrants—whose rights the law should have protected.

My father arranged for my Aunt Fumiko to enter a different college in the Midwest, but before she could finish the paperwork the War Relocation Authority ordered that she be transferred to the Amache camp. Her parents were having medical difficulties, and as a result she was never able to go to college. She packed up two cardboard suitcases that contained all the worldly belongings she had brought from LA, and took a train to Colorado. She was accompanied by an MP armed with a rifle who didn't say a word to her the whole trip. Obviously a potentially dangerous foreign agent.

Fumiko's train was segregated, with whites being instructed to go to the left, to the front of the car, and Blacks to the right. As she explained later:

> Being the last to get on, and trying my best not to seem too confused, I turned to the right following the others to the rear of the car. Before I could sit down, my "protector" the mute MP who seemed very irritated motioned with his rifle for me to turn back, stopping me in the middle of the car. That was my introduction to the deep south.

The Fukuyama family did not get back to Los Angeles until May 1947. The train trip to LA was harrowing. Fumiko had married Joseph Ide while in camp and had a toddler, my cousin Jack. Husband Joe suffered from tuberculosis and had a collapsed lung, which left the family without any income. He had to be transported in a wheelchair along with his father, who was paralyzed after suffering a stroke. Fumiko reported this situation to the War Relocation Authority office in Kansas City, which declared them "indigents" who were no longer welcome in Missouri and who were prohibited from ever returning. As she later said, "I have forgiven the insults of that meeting but have been unable to forget the humiliation."

Fumiko somehow got her family back to Los Angeles, where they had their house but no income. My grandfather was never able to reestablish his hardware store; Uncle Joe went to work for the All Peoples Christian Center in south-central LA as a social worker. It was there that he spent the rest of his career.

So my grandmother Shizu and my Aunt Fumiko found, like Narcissa Cornwall, that the way to California involved death and difficulty and dirt. But they both had a sense of their own inner worth, and that self-respect helped sustain them through difficulties that I never had to experience. Thus was America built.

3

BUILDING THINGS

ALTHOUGH I WRITE ABOUT IDEAS AND TEACH FOR A living, I also like to build things. I came to this realization only after I reached adulthood and started on my career. When I was younger, I was deep into the humanities and never in a million years considered becoming an engineer. Most of the engineers I knew growing up in the late 1960s tended conservative and supported the Vietnam War, and I didn't want anything to do with that. It was only later that I began to appreciate what it was that engineers could accomplish, particularly after my two sons, David and John, became engineering majors and ended up using those skills in their careers.

Engineers are problem solvers. Problem-solving does not have the status or dignity of thinking abstract thoughts, but we would be in a lot of trouble without them because there are a lot of problems.

While I was at the Rand Corporation in the 1980s, I got to know an older German colleague named Konrad Kellen. Konrad had been the novelist Thomas Mann's private secretary and moved with him to Los Angeles when Mann went into exile during the Second World War. Kellen built his Rand career around interrogating German POWs, but also had a hobby of turning bowls and other objects on a lathe. I was tempted to learn woodworking, but worried that if I got into this, it would consume too much time and energy. Nonetheless I made the jump, and didn't emerge until forty years later.

When I joined the State Department in early 1989, my wife, Laura, and I moved from California to northern Virginia, and I built my first woodworking shop. Everyone learns cabinetmaking by starting on Shaker furniture, which is simple, functional, and involves no curves or decoration. I initially built a European-style workbench and a credenza made out of cherry; I built a kitchen table that we still use, and beds for my three children. One of the most pleasurable skills I acquired was learning how to hand-dovetail drawers and case pieces.

After we moved into our own house in McLean, Virginia, I got more serious. The Secretary of State's ceremonial suite on the eighth floor of the State Department is filled with beautiful Federal-style furniture, which I always admired as I walked through delivering memos to the executive secretary's office. The Federal style was a colonial-era American derivative of the English Sheraton and Hepplewhite designs. I could not remotely afford to buy even the reproductions of this furniture, the sort you see in high-end hotels, so I decided to learn how to make them myself. I bought a book by Michael Dunbar on how to build a Federal card table. These are demilune tables with a folding leg that are typically decorated with string inlay and medallions.

My most ambitious project started when a roughly ten-inch-diameter walnut tree fell down in the stream behind our house. I cut it up into three-inch-thick slabs with an Alaskan chainsaw mill—a horrible process involving pushing a large chainsaw down the length of the log, all the while breathing the saw's two-cycle exhaust. These slabs then spent two years drying out, after which I resawed them into thinner boards on a band saw. These I then fashioned into a pair of Federal-style Pembroke tables, which like the card table were decorated with inlays and then French polished. Five years elapsed between the tree falling and the completion of the tables.

I found this project so exhausting that I turned away from woodworking altogether. I reviewed Matt Crawford's *Shop Class as Soulcraft*, in which he lamented how high school shop classes were closing all over the country in favor of computer-based skills such as graphic design, in *The New York Times*. In my very positive review, I mentioned my difficulties selling off my own shop equipment. After the review came out, I got several offers to buy the whole lot. The power tools all left in a big truck a few days later.

One of two Pembroke tables I made from a walnut tree in my backyard

I restarted woodworking a few years later after my wife and I were back in California and purchased a small house in Carmel-by-the-Sea. This gave me an opportunity to reacquire many of the power tools I had sold. A large part of the pleasure I get from hobbies lies in purchasing equipment. I went on to build a set of six Windsor chairs based on the furniture maker Thomas Moser's Bowback design, a project that took four years to complete. I was once again exhausted. But this gave me the excuse to move to a different hobby, flying first-person view (FPV) drones, and acquire a different set of tools.

Building furniture out of wood is very satisfying because it is so tangible. My life has revolved around different forms of intellectual activity: reading, writing, and speaking, dealing with abstractions and ideas. It is often very hard to understand what if anything I've accomplished as a result. This is particularly true of being a teacher. You hope you are strengthening the minds and character of your students, but it is impossible to know just what contribution you've made to their futures. Building beds for my children or chairs or a kitchen table, by contrast, engenders a very different kind of satisfaction because it is so tangible and obviously useful. The material objects you make will also last a while: I imagine my Federal card table will outlast me, and may be handed down to my grandchildren long after they've forgotten about my books.

4

PROFESSORVILLE

I IMAGINE IT WAS FOREORDAINED THAT I WOULD become an academic. My mother's father, Shiro Kawata, was a distinguished professor in Japan, as is my cousin Teiichi Kawata, who like his grandfather became the president of a Japanese university; my father became a professor and an academic dean; and my daughter, Julia, is now a professor as well. While I was growing up, I told myself I didn't want to be a professor and avoided the academic route after getting my PhD. But ending up as an academic was an overdetermined outcome.

I never met my maternal grandfather, Shiro, who died in 1941. He came from a Samurai family and was part of the generation born after the Meiji restoration that sought to modernize Japan and catch up with the West. He was sent as a student to study economics in Germany before the First World War. There he managed to acquire the library of the German sociologist Werner Sombart, which he brought back to Japan. Those books are now in the library of the Osaka Municipal University; I inherited one small part of that collection, a first edition of Karl Marx's *Das Kapital.*

My grandfather's specialty was agricultural economics, but he was also a public intellectual who wrote many books in the course of his career on a wide variety of topics. He was, in the context of Japan in the 1920s and 1930s, very much on the left. He was an early supporter of women's rights and wrote several books on female equality. He was a close friend of Hajime Kawakami, a Marxist professor who was jailed during the 1930s by the military government as a subversive. The two of them are buried close to each other in a cemetery at Honen-in, a beautiful Buddhist temple in Kyoto. My grandfather was a founding member of the economics department at Kyoto University, and went on to become the president of Osaka Municipal University. He had a variety of talents, being a calligrapher and a horseman as well as a writer and teacher.

My cousin Teiichi Kawata was born right at the end of

My maternal grandfather, Professor Shiro Kawata

World War II. His mother, Sumiko, was pregnant with him in 1945 when his father died, which happened in part because he could not get adequate medical attention due to wartime privations. I'm here today because Henry Stimson, Roosevelt's secretary of war, urged the US command to spare Kyoto from firebombing due to the high density of cultural sites there. I remember my mother talking about the sound of B-29s flying over the city on their way to other targets. Sumiko raised Teiichi by herself in postwar Japan; he went on to become a well-known professor of Chinese intellectual history, and eventually the president of Kansai University in Osaka. My cousin is soft-spoken and very kind, and I've stayed in touch with him and his three daughters. I was moved when he told me that he looked at me as a kind of brother, since both of us were only children.

While my mother, Toshiko, came from an academic family, she was a much more physical person, an athlete who later started a pottery business. She grew up in Kyoto as the third of four children and attended Doshisha University, originally a Christian school. The early 1940s were very hard for her: her father died in 1941, and her younger sister, Kazuko, passed away the following year from a heart condition at age twenty-one. Both of her brothers had died by the end of the war, leaving her alone with her mother and her sister-in-law, Sumiko. When I visited Kyoto for the first time as an adult in the early 1980s, I came to realize how incredibly sad those years were for her, quite apart from wartime privations.

My mother was urged to study in the United States and in 1949 began the program at the University of Chicago's School of Social Service Administration. She was one of the first Japanese to come to the United States after the war, and it was

With my mother, Toshiko

rough going. She was given a job as a switchboard operator, not really knowing how to speak English well. But she met and married my father in 1950 and had me in 1952. Their first home was Frank Lloyd Wright's Robie House in Hyde Park, which was then being used by the university as graduate student housing. I have no memory of living there, but my father said that the furniture in the house, designed by Wright himself, was incredibly uncomfortable.

My mother's student visa expired that year, and she had to return with me to Japan, where I spent six months prior to my first birthday. At that time, the quota for Japanese immigrants was only one hundred individuals per year, and it wasn't clear when we would be able to rejoin my father. She was somehow able to return outside the quota system in 1953.

My father grew up working in my grandfather's store—Fukuyama Hardware—in LA's Little Tokyo. His father, Keikichi, was something of a community leader, heading the association of Japanese immigrants from Fukuoka Prefecture. My father, however, had no interest in business—anyway the hardware store was lost during the wartime relocation—but rather wanted to go into the ministry. My grandmother's family had converted to Christianity while still in Japan, and my father volunteered to become a missionary for the Congregational Church (a mainline Protestant denomination, now the United Church of Christ). He went to Turkey in 1945 to teach in a missionary school in Talas, and managed to learn Turkish in the three years he spent there.

Perhaps because of his religious background, my father was a committed liberal and pacifist. He kept a journal during

My father, Dr. Yoshio Fukuyama

his travels to Turkey, during which he passed through North Africa and Palestine before the establishment of the State of Israel. In the journal he kept during those years, he was proud not to have been swept up into the jingoism against Germany and Japan brought on by the war. After he returned to the United States he finished his college education at the same Doane College in Crete, Nebraska, that had welcomed his sister Kiku, then went on to the University of Chicago to attend the Divinity School. He eventually got a PhD in sociology, writing on the sociology of religion. For the first fifteen or so years of his career, he worked for the national board of the United Church of Christ as its research director, doing empirical studies of church members and ministers.

My father remained a diehard liberal his whole life. He and his church were at the forefront of the Civil Rights Movement and opposition to the Vietnam War. I met the theologian and 2024 presidential candidate Cornel West when guest lecturing at Harvard sometime before the Covid pandemic, and was surprised at the warmth with which he remembered my father from the Civil Rights days. I turned more conservative when I left for Cornell and fell under the influence of Allan Bloom and the Straussian crowd, something that pained my father greatly. He didn't understand what had changed in my thinking; he told his friends that one of my professors had gone to work for the Pentagon and "brainwashed" me after returning to academia. I have to admit I occasionally triggered him by saying snide things about the Democrats, something I regret in retrospect in light of the delight that conservatives now take in doing something similar. My views have in any event ended up much more aligned with his as I've gotten older. I nonetheless regret the fact that he never gave me credit for being able to think for myself. Every time I said something he disliked, he attributed my opinions to the fact that I had been brainwashed by someone else. Once, when he and my mother were visiting me and my wife in Santa Monica while I was working at Rand during the 1980s, he asked me, "When are you going to get a real job?"

My father passed away when he was about the age I am now, shortly after the publication of *The End of History and the Last Man*. I'm glad that he got to read the book and see the attention it got, and I often wonder what he would have thought of his son forty years further on.

5

WE HASTEN WITH EAGER STEPS

THERE ARE TWO FACULTIES WITH WHICH NATURE SAW fit not to endow me: athletic ability, and a talent for music. My mother was a superb athlete who might have been able to play tennis professionally had her life circumstances been different, and she continued to play until just before her passing when she was in her early eighties. My father was never so inclined, and for better or worse, I took after him. In our household, traditional gender roles were reversed: my mother spent Sundays watching football on television, while my father grumbled about late dinners and noise from the TV. In middle school gym class, I was one of the slowest runners and was always picked last for teams. My mother once tried to teach me tennis, but gave up after half an hour because I was so bad at it.

I never worried that much about my lack of sports ability but deeply regretted not being able to play an instrument. There was definitely musical talent on the Fukuyama side of the family, and my wife and three children can all play well.

But that gene skipped me. As a seventh grader at the Riverdale Country Day School in New York, I won a prize for the Most Improvement in Music, advancing from a D to a B plus in the course of the year. This proved that even back in the 1960s, no level of incompetence would ever go unrecognized in America.

My music teacher in seventh grade was none other than Peter Schickele of P. D. Q. Bach fame. I had in fact asked my parents to take me to the inaugural P. D. Q. Bach concert at Town Hall in 1965, but I fell sick with the flu that evening and they went by themselves. They told me that Schickele had shimmied down a rope from the balcony and conducted his cantata *Iphigenia in Brooklyn*. I'm not sure that I learned much about music from him that year, despite my Improvement in Music award. The thing I most remember from his class was his inability to keep order in the classroom.

The following year, however, he was replaced by Mr. Wiegand, who knew how to make eighth graders pay attention, and it was from him that I learned the basic sequence of classical music styles from baroque to romantic to twelve-tone and Arnold Schoenberg. (Nobody, of course, enjoys listening to Schoenberg.) He made clear his view that Johann Sebastian Bach was the greatest of all composers, and that the greatest of his compositions were the cantatas he wrote each week as the Kapellmeister at the Thomaskirche in Leipzig.

What really sold me on Bach, however, was a recording he played for us called *Bach's Greatest Hits*. It was done by a French group called the Swingle Singers, led by an American named Ward Swingle. Their early albums were done in the jazz style of wordless scat singing, but performed as note-for-note transcriptions of Bach compositions, accompanied only by a bass and drums to a syncopated beat.

Bach was my favorite composer as an eighth grader, and remains so to this day. We learned about counterpoint from Mr. Wiegand, and the mathematical precision of the timing of the different voices in the fugues of *The Well-Tempered Clavier.* I've come to believe that one of the greatest accomplishments of Western civilization was the five-part choral fugue "Cum Sancto Spiritu" from the B Minor Mass, a piece of such complexity that it has to be witnessed in person to be properly appreciated. The complexity would not have been nearly as impressive, however, were it not for Bach's incredible ear for melody. The Swingle Singers did a transcription of the Sinfonia from Bach's Partita No. 2, in which a single soprano voice carries one of the loveliest extended melodies ever created. My wife, who is also a great fan of Bach but more of a traditionalist, never liked this version. But I always felt it demonstrated how the human voice could be infinitely more expressive than a piano. I am certain that Bach would have greatly preferred this interpretation of his work, sung with a depth of emotion that would have been impossible to replicate on any keyboard in his day.

When my kids were growing up, we listened incessantly on long car trips to cassette tapes featuring the major composers. One that was burned into my head was *Mr. Bach Comes to Call*, in which Johann Sebastian Bach returns to earth and tells a bunch of kids how lucky they are to have access to modern pianos, instead of the harpsichords and claviers with which he had to work. Toward the end of the tape, he is asked what the most favorite of his own compositions is, and he points to a duet from one of his cantatas. And indeed, he was right about this. The soprano-mezzo duet that forms the second movement of Cantata No. 78, "Wir eilen mit schwachen, doch emsigen Schritten" ("We hasten with weak yet eager steps"), brings together melody and counterpoint in an exquisite manner and bids fair to be one of the most beautiful pieces of music ever written.

Listening to music is fundamentally a collective activity, in which diverse listeners are able to experience a common emotional state. You can see this in rock concerts, where fans appear to be in a state of mass hysteria. This is something Socrates notes in Book V of *The Republic*, and why he thinks that music is dangerous. As such, it is closely related to social identity. Societies with long histories usually have deep traditions of music and dance that came out of peasant cultures; hearing them in the present often invokes feelings of patriotism and solidarity.

The United States never evolved out of a peasant society, and lacks these kinds of deep cultural roots. Popular music has become both fragmented and internationalized; teenagers relate to one another according to which sub-sub-genre of music they listen to. Classical music never took root in the United States; its prominence in the mid-twentieth century, when I was born, was due to the thin layer of educated elites who kept it alive. There are few American composers who have contributed to the classical music tradition; youth orchestras today are sustained by the children of Asian immigrants whose parents force them to take Suzuki-method instrument lessons.

To the extent that America has something like a folk music tradition, it lies in the Great American Songbook created in the period from the end of World War I up through the 1940s. I write a tribute to Dorothy Fields, the greatest twentieth-century American songwriter, every year on her birthday in July. Fields was the daughter of a Jewish immigrant named Lew Fields, who became a well-known Broadway producer. His daughter wrote songs with Jimmy McHugh and Jerome Kern such as “I Can’t Give You Anything but Love” and “The Way You Look Tonight” that featured in many of the films of Fred Astaire and Ginger Rogers. American popular music in the nineteenth century, like vaudeville, was, frankly, both hokey and boring. But the big immigration wave that occurred at the turn of the twentieth century led to new influences from African Americans, Latin America, and Jewish songwriters such as Fields, Irving Berlin, and the Gershwins. From that moment on, American identity was built around this kind of multicultural mix. The Great American Songbook fed directly into another uniquely American musical tradition, jazz. I built myself a music server when digital music first appeared, and have perhaps one of the world’s largest collections of music in this genre, a dozen versions each of Billy Strayhorn’s “Lush Life” and Richard Rodgers’s “You Took Advantage of Me.”

Rock ’n’ roll might be seen as the next stage in the evolution of that tradition, but with the Beatles’ appearance on *The Ed Sullivan Show* in 1964 the genre became internationalized and a marker of a broad, global youth culture rather than something uniquely American. The fragmentation of musical genres continued relentlessly, and by the 2010s, music itself had started to get sucked into the country’s broader political polarization. The lack of a strong national musical tradition contributes to the weakness of American national identity. So while I remain a lifetime admirer of Johann Sebastian Bach, I continue to listen to the Great American Songbook, and am all in favor of contemporary artists who want to recast recent songs in that older tradition and keep alive a genuine American culture.

6

THE BEST WAY TO LIVE

IN THE ACADEMIC YEAR THAT BEGAN IN 2023, CAMPUSES all over the United States erupted in protests against Israel's treatment of the Palestinians in Gaza following the Hamas attack on Israel on October 7. Cornell and Stanford were among many universities that saw protest encampments spring up, though both avoided some of the violence and arrests that occurred at Columbia, UCLA, and Harvard.

Student protests escalating into violent confrontations are nothing new. When I arrived as a freshman at Cornell in the fall of 1970, the school was still reeling from the crisis that had broken out the previous spring, during which Willard Straight Hall was occupied by members of the Black student union who were armed with rifles; photographs of them with bandoliers of ammunition strung around their chests appeared on the cover of *Time* magazine. The university had to close down early that spring, and we were given the whole month of January off the following year so that we could do "community service." The issues then were not so different from those in 2023–24; student demands were for an end to the Vietnam War and establishment of a Black

Studies program. Many of the professors in the university's well-known Southeast Asian Studies program were heavily engaged in antiwar opposition.

At Cornell, I lived not in a dormitory but in Telluride House, a fraternity-like building housing a student association that had its own endowment and provided full room and board scholarships to its members. I stumbled on this option by blindly checking a box on the application to take the PSAT exam. I had really wanted to go to Harvard. I didn't have any particular reason for this preference, other than the general prestige of the university. I visited Cambridge in high school and thought it was one of the coolest cities I'd ever seen. There were three of us in my high school class in State College who applied there that year; our interviewer was the father of one of the applicants, and wouldn't you know it, his son was the one who was accepted.

Being rejected by Harvard, it turned out, was a stroke of luck, since my life took a different turn at Cornell.

Telluride at that time was heavily under the influence of the political theorist Allan Bloom. He had been a faculty guest there in the 1960s and had inspired a number of students to pursue graduate studies in political philosophy. In the course of the Cornell crisis, he became disgusted with what he regarded as the weak response of the Cornell administration and its president, James Perkins, in defense of academic freedom. A number of professors were threatened with violence, leading Bloom to resign in protest and move to the University of Toronto. By the time I got to Cornell, Bloom was already in Canada, but he still had to fulfill his teaching contract and thus commuted back to Ithaca each week to lead one final class, a seminar on Plato's *Republic*.

Everyone should begin their undergraduate education in this fashion. If you don't start by thinking about big ideas, you'll never get to them later in life, or your views will be shaped by the unsystematic opinions of people in your social set. *The Republic* is an extended dialogue between the philosopher Socrates and two young aristocratic Athenians, Glaucon and Adeimantus, about the nature of justice. They go through several existing theories of justice, including the view of another interlocutor, Thrasymachus, who argues that justice is nothing more than the "advantage of the stronger"; that is, that might makes right. Socrates demonstrates the weaknesses of these alternative arguments. For example, if justice is nothing more than the advantage of the stronger, how does a band of robbers operate? There must be some principle of justice that allows them to carry out their crimes together without turning on one another.

Socrates then builds a model of a just city "in speech," in which the principle that each person should get their due is realized. The question of what each person deserves leads to an inquiry about human nature. Socrates asks what about humans is due to their shared natures and thus universal, and what is due to customs, habits, or what we today would call "culture." He suggests that there are indeed certain characteristics that are natural, such as a human being's ability to reason, and the desires for food and drink shared by all people. He also notes that there is a third part of the soul—what Socrates labels *thymos*, or spiritedness—that desires something intangible, the respect or esteem of other human beings. Other human characteristics—their language, their clothing, the kind of food they eat—are not natural but the result of customs.

In this discussion, Plato through the mouth of Socrates raises questions that continue to be relevant to the present day. For example, the model of human behavior posited by contemporary neoclassical economics is that human beings are "rational utility maximizers," who are driven primarily by their material needs. This captures the first two parts of the soul—rationality and desire—but it misses *thymos* entirely, and therefore cannot comprehend the desire for nonmaterial recognition that drives much of modern identity politics on both the left and the right. Socrates might call into question a central tenet of identity politics, which is the denial of human universals and the belief that "lived experiences" of different races, ethnicities, and genders make mutual comprehension hard if not impossible.

In another dialogue, the *Apology*, Socrates has been accused of poisoning the minds of young Athenians through his philosophical inquiries, and has been condemned to death. His perpetual questioning of received wisdom, and particularly his questioning of the community's religious beliefs, has been held to undermine Athenian society. He is asked in effect to recant his life, which he refuses to do. Rather, he says, his life has been spent trying to understand what is the best way to live, for himself and for other human beings. He has concluded that the happiest life lies in rational self-understanding: "The unexamined life is not worth living." He is then forced to swallow hemlock.

Allan Bloom believed that a liberal education needed to begin with big questions like these: What is the best way to live, what makes for the highest forms of human happiness, what is the nature of justice, what is natural and what is conventional in human affairs? People living in contemporary liberal democracies tend to imbibe an easygoing kind of relativism: they don't believe that there is such a thing as "the truth," they don't think that any particular moral perspective is better than any other, and they don't want to be "judgmental," since that implies believing that your own moral standpoint is superior to those of others. We may come to such opinions eventually as a condition for living in a liberal society, but they should not be assumptions we accept unquestioningly.

Many years after I left Cornell, Bloom published a book that became a big bestseller, *The Closing of the American Mind*. It was written in response to the first wave of identity politics and postmodernist critiques of the Western canon. Many schools in the early twentieth century had developed Western civilization core courses that began with the Hebrew Bible and Greek philosophy, continuing through thinkers such as Machiavelli; Hobbes; Rousseau; and Hamilton, Madison, and Jay in *The Federalist Papers*, up through more modern figures such as Marx and Freud.

These kinds of curricula became the target of activists in the late 1980s: Jesse Jackson came to Stanford University in 1987 and attended a rally where students chanted, "Hey hey, ho ho, Western culture's got to go." Classics such as those of Plato and Aristotle were dismissed as foundations of a white, Eurocentric patriarchy, and virtually every elite university began to dismantle its Western civilization core curriculum in favor of a multicultural one.

In many respects this reform was long overdue. Young people should be exposed early on to other civilizations: China, the Islamic world, and Hinduism all provide alternative framings of the human condition and directly shape the world that students will encounter in their future lives. The historical narrative on which Western Civ classes were based often embedded a form of so-called Whig history, in which the human experience was reduced to a progressive narrative of the Anglo-Saxon world's unimpeded progress toward an egalitarian liberal economic and political order. Phenomena such as slavery, patriarchy, and colonialism were swept under the rug.

Yet in subsequent years virtually every elite school threw the baby out with the bathwater. In accepting the premise that students ought to know something about non-Western cultures as part of their undergraduate educations, universities found it impossible to make distinctions between more and less important forms of cultural knowledge, or to honestly confront cultural differences. Exposure to philosophical debates about the fundamental nature of justice or human happiness had no priority over knowledge of queer culture in seventeenth-century Spain or varieties of Polynesian cuisine. There was a hidden premise underlying the then burgeoning field of multiculturalism that non-Western and/or premodern cultures in the end were more liberal and tolerant than contemporary Western societies. There was a widespread view among anthropologists, for example, that indigenous cultures were less violent and more responsible stewards of the environment than their modern capitalist counterparts.

Multiculturalism was fused from the beginning with a social justice agenda. It was never intended to truly educate students about alternative cultures and open their minds to seeing things through a non-Western lens. Rather, it was meant to raise the dignity and self-respect of cultures that had been marginalized in a world dominated by Western values and institutions. This could not be done, evidently, without denigrating the latter. Social justice activism thus inevitably clashed with the university's core function as a knowledge-generating institution built around freedom of thought.

There was nothing wrong with multiculturalism if done honestly. But the kind of studies promoted in universities quietly reinjected Western values into the understanding of non-Western societies: in the end, all societies were seen to be tolerant, peaceful, and environmentally conscious, to an even greater extent than the United States. What students never got was a genuine confrontation with cultural difference: that some societies prized hierarchy and cruelty, that holding the wrong religious beliefs would merit death, or that the stronger should rule the weaker.

What I got from my formal education was similar to what an upper-class European would have received in the nineteenth century: a firm grounding in the Greek and Latin classics, and a broad knowledge of the philosophical tradition that led from there up to the present. That grounding did not begin with the assumption that democracy and liberalism were obviously the best ways to organize a society. Rather, the classics considered other forms of government such as aristocracy and tyranny; knowledge of the moderns provided an understanding of how liberalism emerged as an alternative to pre-liberal and pre-egalitarian politics.

One of the greatest students of modern democracy, Alexis de Tocqueville, was himself an aristocrat and was aware of what was lost with the transition to an egalitarian society. In book II, part 1, of *Democracy in America*, a chapter devoted to the intellectual shortcomings of democratic America, he expresses an appreciation for a society both hierarchical and deeply religious that could produce a figure like Blaise Pascal:

> If Pascal had had nothing in view but some large gain, or even if he had been stimulated by the love of fame alone, I cannot conceive that he would ever have been able to rally all the powers of his mind, as he did, for the better discovery of the most hidden things of the Creator. When I see him, as it were, tear his soul from the midst of all the cares of life to devote it wholly to these researches and, prematurely snapping the links which bind the frame to life, die of old age before forty, I stand amazed, and I perceive that no ordinary cause is at work to produce efforts so extra-ordinary.

Wrestling with a thinker such as Pascal who takes religion seriously and does not accept some of the premises of our contemporary liberal consensus is what it means to be exposed to diversity of thought.

After the 1980s identity politics went quiescent for a while and moved underground. A liberal education came to be threatened from another side, which was the laser-like focus of students and their parents on job skills that would earn them secure employment for the rest of their lives. The study of big, important questions was not what employers were looking for in résumés, and liberal arts curricula were pushed to the side. Bloom once said that he liked interacting with the left-wing students of the 1960s more than with the careerist drones of later decades; the former were at least serious about ideas.

Not to worry; identity politics was not defeated but simply burrowed deeper into the sinews of humanities programs around the country. This was particularly true of literature departments, which turned away from reading texts for the wisdom they may contain to a social justice agenda. I suspect this happened because they, unlike the social sciences, were removed from any grounding in empirical reality, and were free to indulge in fantasies of what a perfectly just world would look like.

In the third decade of the twenty-first century, identity politics made a big comeback, particularly after the killing of George Floyd during the Covid pandemic in 2020. In many ways, the movement had regressed since the 1980s. Back then, there was a prolonged and sophisticated debate over the sources of African American poverty, in which factors such as culture, family structure, and bad policy incentives played a role in locking people into an "underclass." The 2020s version promoted DEI (diversity, equity, and inclusion). The substitution of the word "equity" for "equality" in contemporary social justice discourse was driven by the assumption that any difference in outcomes between social groups was attributable simply to racism or patriarchy. Outcomes were now divorced from individual choice and attributed to social structure. The progressive emphasis on identity then stimulated a huge backlash on the part of conservatives, some of whom began portraying themselves as victims of a broad left-wing conspiracy. The counterattack on "wokeness" and DEI under the second Trump administration was so extreme and exaggerated that it made any reasonable discussion of the strengths and weaknesses of identity politics impossible.

For me, one of the worst aspects of progressive identity politics was the way that it made it very difficult, especially at elite universities, to provide the kind of liberal education that I enjoyed. As a freshman, I was made to wrestle with the problem of "what is the best way to live" or "what is justice" at the start of my higher education. This is not to minimize the importance of social justice concerns. But they have to be both placed in the context of a broader philosophical discussion of the nature of justice per se, as well as enriched with a more detailed understanding of the present historical context. To dismiss Plato and Aristotle as "white males" and replace them on the required reading list with the Guatemalan indigenous activist Rigoberta Menchú is to deprive students of what might be a transformative moment in their educations. This was the message of *The Closing of the American Mind*, and it remains valid to the present.

This is what I learned from Allan Bloom, and from the other teachers I had as an undergraduate.

7

ALLAN BLOOM

ONE OF THE BIG PROBLEMS WITH AMERICAN CONSERVA-tives and particularly those of a libertarian bent is their focus on individualism, and their failure to recognize how each individual is shaped by the society that surrounds them. Those youthful readers of Ayn Rand would like to believe that heroic geniuses spring from the ground like gods and master the universe exclusively through their own talent and will. Individual ability and character are important, of course, but those people who rise to the top in a hypercompetitive society like that of the United States tend to think too highly of themselves. They don't understand the ways in which sheer luck led them to privilege and produced the outcomes that their lives come to embody.

I've long felt that I am one of the luckiest people alive in terms of the teachers I've had. There were four in particular who were crucial: Allan Bloom, whom I met my first semester at Cornell; Harvey Mansfield, with whom I studied in graduate school at Harvard; Samuel Huntington, who became a mentor after I had graduated; and finally Seymour Martin

Lipset, who was critical in teaching me about American politics, as well as in helping me to get my first academic position.

It is very hard to describe to those who never met him exactly what made Allan Bloom such a charismatic teacher. Most descriptions of his "lifestyle" leave listeners—and particularly women—cold: he comes off as a materialistic, pretentious, affected dandy. His close friend Saul Bellow tried to portray him in his novel *Ravelstein*, but in my view didn't fully succeed. I can only try to convey this through my personal experiences with him.

Bloom had a circle of students inside and outside of Telluride House, a number of whom followed him up to Toronto for graduate study. Bloom stayed at the House as a faculty guest on these visits, and he would hold forth in discussions of Plato, Aristotle, Rousseau, and every other conceivable topic late at night in the ground-floor Telluride kitchen.

Bloom had a nervous stutter and would punctuate his talk repeatedly with "the ah, the ah, the ah . . ." as he searched for the right phrase. But he was magnificent as a lecturer, talking with no notes and stopping exactly at the assigned length of time. He smoked heavily and his students would watch anxiously as the ash on his cigarette grew longer and longer, wondering when it would fall on his immaculately tailored suit.

I reconnected with Bloom only in the mid-1980s when he had left Toronto for the University of Chicago's Committee on Social Thought. My parents had themselves moved to Hyde Park from Pennsylvania when my father got a job as the academic dean of the Chicago Theological Seminary. They lived in a town house on Fifty-Eighth Street that was catty-corner to the Cloisters, where both Bloom and Saul Bellow lived. At that time I was working in Santa Monica at Rand. I made the strange decision to visit my parents at Christmastime, when it was in the seventies in LA and minus twenty degrees in Chicago. I spent a lot of time in Bloom's apartment and met Bellow, who was almost always present. Bloom didn't drive, and was constantly asking me to chauffeur him somewhere in my parents' car. It was an old Buick; Chicago in that period hadn't yet come out of the big crime wave of the 1980s, and my father had to get a special plate installed around the trunk lock so thieves couldn't bore it out.

Bloom was an obsessive consumer of many things. He had an expensive espresso machine, which in those years had not yet become a de rigueur middle-class accessory. He had a massive collection of more than four thousand vinyl records, together with a pricey Linn Sondek turntable. I had at that point developed an interest in high-end stereo, though I could not remotely afford any of the equipment that got reviewed in *The Absolute Sound* or *Stereophile.*

One day I showed up at Bloom's apartment and all of his records were gone, leaving yards of empty shelves. The CD player had just been invented, and he started on a manic effort to reacquire his entire record collection in this new format. He said CDs were great; they didn't get scratched and he didn't have to worry about dropping cigarette ashes on them.

A few months later I met him in Paris, where he spent a good part of the year. He was buying up every CD he could get his hands on. We met in a CD store where he had emptied out the inventory. After coffee at the café Les Deux Magots on the Boulevard Saint-Germain, we returned to the store and he asked the proprietor whether any more CDs had come in during the hour we spent in the café. Yes, M. Bloom, two more had just arrived! He bought them without even looking to see their titles.

The following year back in Chicago he proudly showed me his new stereo equipment, which as I remember included a pair of expensive Krell power amplifiers. I exclaimed, "What, Mr. Bloom, no tubes?" His face fell and he said, "Tubes? What are tubes?" I explained that the best power amplifiers used Russian vacuum tubes rather than power transistors, and that no self-respecting audiophile would be caught dead with a solid-state amp. The next week, the Krells were gone, replaced by a pair of big Audio Research tube monoblocks that easily cost more than $10,000 in 1985 currency. When I told my friend Abe—who had also been one of Bloom's students—this had happened, he got agitated. He explained that he had lent Bloom money as a graduate student, and now would never get it back. In this period before *The Closing of the American Mind* became a big bestseller, Bloom perpetually spent money he didn't have so that he could be surrounded by fine things—or as Bellow corrected, "not necessarily fine things, but expensive things." He was, in Bellow's words, "throwing money out the back of a truck."

Looking back on Bloom's life and behavior, I find it hard to explain to those who never met him why his students considered him so admirable. Habits that would be considered vices in other people were readily excused by his followers because of his charisma. His behavior was certainly unusual: none of his students had met an academic anything remotely like him, with his expensive tastes and seeming disregard for ordinary things such as money or cigarette ashes. There was an authenticity to his eccentricities—I don't think anyone would have believed that his ticks and manias were an act that he put on to impress people. He took great personal interest in students he thought had great philosophical potential, but could be biting and dismissive of those he felt didn't measure up.

Bloom had his share of critics, and not simply reviewers of his books. He had almost no female students and took little interest in them. The spouses and girlfriends of his students tended to have a rather jaundiced view of him. He died of AIDS in 1992; it was a mark of my own naïveté that I didn't realize he was gay until that moment. He was very discreet about his sexuality and I never heard any hint of inappropriate behavior toward his many male students. He had a habit of picking favorites, and deciding that one student or another was truly brilliant and disposed toward philosophy, while others were not. People who were not within that charmed circle were naturally resentful and felt that there was a cultish quality to it, with protégés adopting his quirks and gestures and ways of speaking.

I decided early on that I didn't have what it took to be a serious student of philosophy, and in any event did not want to pursue an academic career, which was the only available path for someone doing a graduate program in political theory. Nonetheless, an appreciation for truly philosophical thought is a gift of inestimable value that remains with you for a lifetime.

8

WHO WAS LEO STRAUSS?

SO WHO WAS LEO STRAUSS, ALLAN BLOOM'S TEACHER? He was clearly one of the most important intellectual influences in my life, despite the fact that I never met him.

Strauss was a German Jew who fled Hitler's Europe and ended up teaching at a number of American universities, primarily the University of Chicago, which was where Allan Bloom studied with him. Another of my mentors, Harvey Mansfield, was heavily influenced by him. Strauss died in 1973 while I was still in college, so I never got a chance to meet him in person. But he nonetheless heavily shaped the course of my education.

At the time of the Iraq War, a lot of nonsense was written about Strauss, largely because Paul Wolfowitz, one of the war's architects, was influenced by Strauss through his connection with Allan Bloom. Strauss said virtually nothing about contemporary politics or foreign policy; he was, first and foremost, a careful reader of other philosophers. His major books were interpretations of Maimonides, Hobbes, Machiavelli, al-Farabi, Xenophon, Spinoza, Plato, and many others. Those interpretations were dense and complex, and required going back to the original text to understand them.

Leo Strauss's central concern was what he called the "crisis of modernity." The Western philosophical project started with Plato and Aristotle, who sought to use reason to study the most important human things, such as the best way to live and the nature of justice. The great philosophers were in conversation with one another, and their ideas developed over time. Strauss argued that an important break occurred in the early sixteenth century with Machiavelli, who argued that the horizon of politics as defined by classical thinkers such as Plato and Aristotle needed to be lowered from cultivation of the good life to the protection of life itself. This project was then expanded by early modern liberal thinkers such as Hobbes, Locke, and Rousseau. As I will explain in a subsequent chapter, they differed among themselves on the nature of human nature, yet they all agreed that the preservation of life itself needed to be prioritized over pursuit of the good life. In their day, the good life was defined by organized religion, and the politics of Europe was roiled by competing religious doctrines embraced by ambitious princes.

This modern form of politics, according to Strauss, continued to evolve; G. F. W. Hegel, in particular, explicitly laid out a historicist understanding of human thought, in which earlier forms of consciousness were superseded by later ones. He built on Rousseau's concept of human perfectibility, and argued that history itself was progressive and had evolved to a final point of rationality, an end of history. In the next generation Karl Marx accepted the idea of a progressive history, but maintained that the true end of history was not the liberal state and bourgeois society that emerged after the French Revolution, but rather a Communist utopia that would abolish the injustice of class oppression. It was not a long step from there to Friedrich Nietzsche, who by the end of the nineteenth century posited that there was no end of history, and that ideas were simply reflections of an underlying, never-ending will to power. He and Martin Heidegger were, in Strauss's view, the codifiers of the crisis of modernity, who could say, as Nietzsche did, that "there are no facts, only interpretations." The connection to contemporary postmodernist thought is clear: claims to truth or to "master narratives" are not grounded in reason or empirical reality; rather, they are structures that express the will and justify the oppressive actions of existing power holders. This was true not just of philosophical thought but of the Enlightenment's project of understanding the world through modern natural science.

The Western tradition of philosophical reason had thus ended up undermining itself. When combined with a liberalism that prized tolerance above all virtues, it led to an easygoing relativism in which all points of view were equally true and valid. The effect was to discredit all doctrines, including liberalism itself. In the early twentieth century, that liberalism was challenged by other strong ideas such as Communism and fascism, and found itself unable to defend the principles (such as natural rights) on which it was founded.

Strauss was not a conservative who believed that the antidote to modern relativism was a return to belief in a single absolute truth, as is the case for many religious believers. Rather, he urged his students to continue the Socratic project of reasoned dialogue as a way of achieving a higher level of understanding of the human condition. In particular, he argued against the modern conceit of intellectual progress, the idea that older ideas are necessarily superseded by more recent ones. In *Persecution and the Art of Writing*, he argued that many thinkers of the past hid their true thoughts through the use of esoteric writing that required a special interpretive effort to understand. The first thing a student of Strauss learns is not to casually dismiss an older philosophical text simply because it seems to be a "product of its time," but to try to understand the deeper meaning that the writer might have been simultaneously trying to express and yet hide. Above all, he encouraged his students to be open to ideas, and not to assume that something on today's cutting edge is necessarily superior to what came before.

Strauss's views of liberalism were complex. He was in no way an authoritarian, as some of his critics charged; he understood and appreciated how liberal America had protected him from Nazi concentration camps. And yet he was not a committed liberal who believed, like Karl Popper, in the virtues of an "open society." He characterized John Locke's emphasis on property and accumulation as the "joyless search for joy" that had lowered human horizons and blunted the quest for virtue and excellence. This allowed him to understand, in a way that committed liberals could not, why many young people in his day disliked the liberal society in which they lived, and why they were drawn to doctrines such as National Socialism in the search for something that seemed more noble.

Given Strauss's understanding of the evolution of philosophy, it is clear why he had problems with Hegel's historicism, as well as with the account of Hegel provided by

Alexandre Kojève, Hegel's great midcentury Russian-French interpreter. And indeed, they confronted each other directly in a series of letters, and in competing commentaries on Xenophon's dialogue between the tyrant Hiero of Syracuse and the philosopher Simonides. Strauss argued that philosophy and politics were ultimately incompatible because philosophers would always raise questions that would be corrosive of the regimes they lived under. The activity of philosophy moreover sought to understand what was unchanging over time about human beings as a result of their embeddedness in nature. Kojève by contrast believed that human beings were not anchored in nature but could through their own agency change themselves; or perhaps, if they had natures, those natures were perfectible over historical time. I don't remotely have the space or ability to give a proper account of that debate, except to say that it demonstrated the degree to which Strauss took seriously Kojève's historicist point of view, and his specific reasons for rejecting it. That rejection lay ultimately in Strauss's observation that the state of universal recognition posited by Kojève as the end of history was the domain of Nietzsche's Last Man, and would not be as humanly satisfying as he suggested.

My own view is that there is a middle ground between the Strauss and Kojève positions, and indeed that middle ground is what I tried to elaborate in *The End of History and the Last Man*. That is, there is undeniably a larger historical process in which human beings can deliberately alter their social conditions as well as their own natures, and this has resulted in huge changes over time in both politics and society. But there is also such a thing as human nature, a core set of faculties and inclinations that ultimately serve to limit human autonomy and ensure that there is continuity in the human experience over time.

Many of my closest friends from university days became "Straussians," in the sense that they studied with Strauss or one of his students, such as Allan Bloom or Harvey Mansfield, and then became professors of political theory themselves. I have great admiration for them, since they have taken seriously the challenge of confronting big ideas and teaching young people how to aspire to think beyond their immediate time and place.

But absorbing Leo Strauss's ideas always had some important downsides. Many people outside the Strauss tradition blamed it for having a cultish quality, fed by Strauss's teaching about esotericism. It was easy for insiders to think that they were a small group privy to a kind of secret knowledge not available to other people. Strauss always made a sharp distinction between people he considered true philosophers, and others who were simply philosophy teachers or intellectual historians (which included the vast majority of people teaching in philosophy departments around the world). This also placed limitations on the ambitions of his second- and third-generation students. They got tenure by publishing close readings of yet another Platonic dialogue or a slightly new take on Hobbes or Machiavelli, and ceased trying to wrestle with big ideas on their own. As Mark Lilla, a recovering Straussian, once remarked, they were like craftsmen building a house brick by brick on a foundation that Leo Strauss had laid. But they would never become architects of that house, or they would decide that the house was too small for them to comfortably live in. Moreover, Strauss disparaged social science and what he considered naive forms of positivism prevalent in American universities. This led some of his followers to disdain merely empirical accounts of current events. If you are more of a Hegelian, you need to pay attention to actual history if you are to give an account of how ideas play out in the real world.

The cultish character of many of Strauss's followers affected the broader American political debate since the rise of Donald Trump. Second-generation students of Strauss were divided for many years between the "East Coast" students of Allan Bloom or Harvey Mansfield, and the "West Coast" acolytes of Harry Jaffa. Jaffa, a political theorist at Claremont McKenna College, wrote an excellent book on the Lincoln-Douglas debates, but went on to cultivate the view that the American Founding Fathers had created a regime that was the apotheosis of Aristotelian virtue. Whatever one may say critically about Leo Strauss himself, he was never an American nationalist, and yet an America-first point of view came to characterize many West Coast Straussians. With the rise of Trump, the Claremont Institute emerged as one of the intellectual centers trying to devise a highbrow defense of Trumpism, spawning characters such as Michael Anton (author of the famous "Flight 93" article), Michael Pack, and John Eastman (who was heavily involved in attempting to overturn the 2020 election). The East Coast Straussians tended not to self-identify as such, and a number, including my old friends Bill Kristol and Bill Galston, went on to become passionate Never Trumpers.

This politicization of Strauss's legacy is very unfortunate. Strauss was far from being any kind of political advocate; he did not believe that philosophy and politics were compatible, or that philosophers had any duty or ability to change the world. It is hard to know what he would make of America's current political situation, but he was certainly never an advocate of noble lies or untrammeled executive power. The person who believed in the power of philosophical ideas was Alexandre Kojève, who lived out his beliefs by becoming a bureaucrat in the predecessor to the European Union, the European Economic Community. Strauss remained to the end a teacher, and a careful reader of philosophical books.

9

ME AND MY UNCLE

IN THE SPRING OF 1974, WHEN I WAS LIVING IN THE Montmartre neighborhood of Paris, there was an unexpected knock at the door. It was my Uncle Hiroo, my father's twin brother, whom I had not seen since we lived in New York in the early 1960s. At that time he was based in Dallas and ran a travel agency. Our prior encounters had been at family dinners in New York when I was a child. These occasions were not entirely pleasant, since his German wife, Christa, had a drinking problem and would often dissolve into angry rants about the Communists in East Germany.

Uncle Hiroo and I went out that evening for drinks. He surprised me with very frank stories of his time in Europe when he was working as a contractor for the US Army, and told me where the prostitutes hung out near the Place Pigalle. This was the first and only time I was able to talk to him one-on-one as an adult. He and my father were at that point alienated from each other, a low point in what had been a painful relationship their whole lives.

I felt sorry for Uncle Hiroo over the years: though he and my father were fraternal twins, my father was always treated as the eldest son by their parents, a traditional role in Japanese families. My father was taller, did better in school, and went on to get a PhD and become a successful academic. My uncle Hiroo by contrast worked as a buyer for the army after leaving the service, then started a travel business and went into other, not terribly successful ventures.

In later years I learned much more about Uncle Hiroo, who turned out to be a far more interesting person than anyone in the family realized at the time. Hiroo had been incarcerated in Camp Amache in Colorado with my grandparents as part of the Japanese internment during the war. Hiroo got out of camp by enlisting in the US Army; he had to sneak out of camp late at night because many of the internees resented the young men volunteering to fight for the country that had imprisoned them.

My Uncle Hiroo being inducted into the US Army

Hiroo joined a military intelligence unit and was sent to the China-Burma theater to work as an interpreter interrogating Japanese POWs. He somehow ended up—apparently—in Chongqing, to which the Nationalist government had evacuated after the Japanese attack on their former seat in Nanjing. There he got to know Soong Ching-ling, widow of the founder of the Chinese Nationalist movement, or Kuomintang, Dr. Sun Yat-sen.

Madame Sun Yat-sen, as she was then known, was the middle sister of three women who became famous in twentieth-century Chinese history. Her older sister, Soong Ei-ling, married a businessman and became one of the richest women in China. Her family became the primary target of cascading corruption charges against the Nationalist government in later years. The youngest sister, Soong Mei-ling, would go on to marry Generalissimo Chiang Kai-shek, the iron-fisted leader of the Kuomintang government that would decamp to Taiwan following defeat by the Communists in 1949. All three sisters were Christians who were educated in the United States and could speak fluent English.

My uncle befriended the middle sister, Soong Ching-ling, who was known as the "Red Sister." She had spent time in Moscow during the 1920s and worked as an agent of the Communist International (Comintern), and played an important role in transmitting information and orders between the Soviets and the fledgling Chinese Communist Party (CCP). The CCP and Kuomintang were forced into an uncomfortable anti-Japanese alliance after the Japanese invasion of Manchuria, and Soong Ching-ling openly detested her brother-in-law Chiang Kai-shek. After the CCP's victory in 1949, she moved to Beijing and went on to play an important role in the

Soong Ching-ling (Madame Sun Yat-Sen), honorary president of the People's Republic of China, in a photo she gave my Uncle Hiroo

People's Republic of China (PRC). She served as vice chair of the National People's Congress, and was elevated to be honorary president of the PRC shortly before her death in 1981. Her younger sister, Madame Chiang Kai-shek, meanwhile rose to considerable power and influence in the Nationalist government in Taiwan. She secured substantial support for the Republic of China from the United States, but also became an object of criticism as a key player in a government known for its corruption and authoritarianism.

Soong Ching-ling, the Red Sister, wrote a number of letters to Uncle Hiroo in the period after he left China for the United States and then Berlin. At that time he was still an enlisted man in his mid-twenties; she was a widow in her early fifties. Several of her letters are very affectionate and personal.

In a letter from after the Japanese surrender in 1945, she wrote:

> Dear Hiroo:
>
> It was a great disappointment to me that I missed the pleasure of seeing you when you dropped in. Particularly since you had failed to turn up at my one and only really enjoyable celebration for the end of the war . . .
>
> Thank you most heartily for your very lovely Victory Gifts. You must come and have a private celebration with me, any evening during the next week. Only please phone me a day ahead so that we can prepare something special.
>
> With warm greetings,
> Yours ever,
> SCL

In another letter written in 1946 after Hiroo had left China, she wrote:

> Tell me everything, how you spend your time and what you read for I am so interested. And don't forget to ask about my letter for I spent quite a long time typing you . . . Even some snapshots of my garden and the kitten that you helped to rescue from the cold garden one evening. Remember? Well, those penciled scrawls you made in the wash room are still kept there as a souvenir . . .
>
> With much love,
> Yours affectionately,
> SCL

None of these communications necessarily show that Soong Ching-ling and Uncle Hiroo had any deeper relationship, as she apparently dealt similarly with a host of younger American visitors in earlier years. Hiroo never talked about her to his family as far as I know. I would, however, very much like to believe that they had been lovers.

My grandmother and Hiroo wrote to each other frequently after he left for the army. Her tone was always upbeat and optimistic, even when she was having all of her teeth extracted by the camp dentist. She remarked on the beauty of the sunsets and flowers and interactions with the other families interned at Amache. She was very proud of Hiroo; there is a picture of her with the other Blue Star Banner mothers whose sons had volunteered for the US military at Camp Amache. In later years, the 442nd Regimental Combat Team, composed entirely of Japanese Americans, would be widely celebrated for their fighting against the Germans in Italy. Being a veteran of the 442nd would launch the career of Senator Daniel Inouye of Hawaii.

At the time, however, not everyone was celebrating these soldiers. As my Aunt Fumiko explained in a 1943 letter to Hiroo:

> You have probably heard about the Jim Crow troop being organized for nisei [second-generation Japanese American] fellows. There has been much discussion along that line here in these camps—the consensus seems to be that this new order has all eligible nisei fellows up a tree. If they do not volunteer, then they are not patriotic or loyal. If they do volunteer, then they will be stuck in an all-Japanese unit. The boys want to fight side by

> side with Americans of all extractions. They don't want to be treated any differently from other soldiers . . . It is branding the nisei as being unable to assimilate with other races.

Even as they tried to prove their loyalty to the United States, the residents of Amache were subject to small daily indignities and suspicions. And some, like my father, Yoshio, had deep reservations about the war itself. There was no trail of correspondence between him and my grandmother as there was with Hiroo. My father had become a Christian pacifist and spent the war years pursuing his education in Nebraska and Chicago.

And no one knew that Hiroo Fukuyama was a bit player and participant in the larger geopolitical struggle taking place at that time.

10

LEICAS AND NIKONS

MY FAMILY MOVED INTO A TWO-BEDROOM APARTMENT in New York's Stuyvesant Town in the mid-1950s, and that is where I grew up. Stuyvesant Town was a massive housing development owned at the time by Metropolitan Life, with some eighty thousand units; it was, and still is, a wonderful middle-class enclave on Manhattan's east side, between Fourteenth and Twenty-Third Streets.

My father had a stash of *Playboy* magazines that he thought were well hidden among his books, but which I discovered early on. While I of course was drawn to the centerfolds, my most vivid memory of the magazine in those years was actually a spread they did on high-end cameras. The photography was done as beautifully as that of any of the women in the issue; there were pictures of a Nikon F, a Leica M3, a Hasselblad, a Bronica, all shot straight on against a white background looking through the lens. These cameras were impossibly expensive, even for my father at the time, and I constantly fantasized about owning one someday.

This dream materialized in later years. While living in Virginia in the early 2000s, I was contacted by a German woman named Katharina who lived in Berlin. She asked whether I was related to Hiroo Fukuyama; I told her that indeed, he was my uncle. Katharina was the niece of Christa, the German woman my uncle had married in Berlin, where he was stationed after the war. She was an artist who did wonderful paintings in the manner of Edward Hopper, which she displayed in a "Fukuyama Gallery" in Berlin.

Hiroo's wife, Christa, was spirited and opinionated, and owned a house in Kleinmachnow, a suburb of Potsdam, to which they lost access once Germany was divided after the war. Hiroo and Christa never had children, and after Hiroo died at the age of sixty-six following a stroke, Christa moved back to Berlin, where niece Katharina took care of her until her passing.

Katharina came to visit us in McLean sometime in the early 2000s, bearing a gift: a pristine Leica M3 that had belonged to my uncle, one that he acquired while living in Berlin. The M3 was a classic produced in Wetzlar, Germany, during the 1950s, so the camera was approximately as old as I was.

There are a lot of ways that an analog film camera is superior to modern digital ones. The main advantage is reliability and longevity. This Leica M3 can still take beautiful thirty-five-millimeter photos in 2025; I guarantee that no digital camera produced today will be usable in the year 2095. The other thing is the film: before I switched completely to digital photography in the late 2000s, I used Kodak Ektachrome E100 almost exclusively, which like Paul Simon's famous Kodachrome produced deeply saturated color transparencies.

I never got into collecting Leicas, which is a bottomless rabbit hole, but I now have a collection of historical film

Nikons. When I earned my first commission writing an article for *Commentary* in 1978, I immediately blew it on a black Nikon F2a, which at that time was the premier professional camera used by photographers all over the world.

Thirty-five-millimeter film had amazing longevity as the leading photographic storage medium for more than fifty years, and has continued to be a niche product well into the twenty-first century. However, the speed of technological advance has been astonishing. The introduction of full-frame digital cameras by Sony about a decade ago has knocked Nikon and Canon off their perch as the duopoly catering to the professional market; the latest Sony digital sensors are so sensitive they can basically see in the dark.

But unfortunately we're at the end of a road for still photography, both on the hardware and creative sides. With the development of smartphones, no one except professional photographers and obsessive hobbyists buys cameras any longer. Nikon's business model is severely threatened, while Leica continues to produce ridiculously expensive cameras that become instant collector's items.

I always preferred photography to painting as a visual art form, because a photograph recorded something that someone actually saw, and thus had a more direct connection with lived reality than a painting. However, the authenticity of photographs has come under increasing challenge ever since the invention of Adobe Photoshop. The challenge grows much deeper with generative AI, which in a sense takes the entire corpus of the world's photographs and digests it into a single large language model. In the future photos may no longer be accepted as documentary evidence in legal proceedings because they are so easy to fake. Video has become far easier to take and edit, and has been rapidly displacing still photography as an activity for hobbyists. It is hard not to believe that still photography as an art form has reached its own local end of history, with every conceivable innovation having been tried by someone over the years.

11

AFTER MODERNITY

FRENCH POSTMODERNISM HIT CORNELL UNIVERSITY like a freight train in the early 1970s. We had a series of visitors—Michel Foucault, Julia Kristeva, Tzvetan Todorov—who were all part of the movement. Foucault stayed at Telluride House during his visit. While I didn't attend his lecture, I do have a memory of him disappearing upstairs to his room one weekend with a group of young men in tow. Cornell hired a couple of professors preaching the new doctrine. One was an apostle of the pscyhoanalyst Jacques Lacan and French Freudianism. The other was a literature professor who wanted to show how cool he was by roasting a whole pig for us, but even after two days on the spit, it was undercooked and inedible.

Postmodernism was a direct offspring of Friedrich Nietzsche and Martin Heidegger and exemplars of Strauss's "crisis of modernity" that had turned everyone into relativists. Nietzsche opened the door to a radical skepticism, not just of traditional religion but of the entire Enlightenment framework of liberalism and modern natural science. Nietzsche was scornful of both Christianity and the egalitarianism that was born from it. He was accused of being a Nazi precursor; Martin

Heidegger was, by contrast, an actual Nazi, having joined the party while rector of the University of Freiburg in the early 1930s. He never disavowed this choice, even after the end of the war. Strauss had come to terms with modern liberalism as a refugee from Hitler's Europe; for him modernity's crisis lay in the fact that people no longer believed in liberalism and were susceptible to the totalitarian value systems ravaging Europe. In a world where there was no truth, anything was now permitted.

This was the beginning of "deconstructionism," which built on the thought of Nietzsche and Heidegger. Strauss argued that many great philosophers wrote esoterically and required close reading to understand the deeper truth that they pointed to. Deconstructionism did the opposite: it used close reading to understand how texts themselves belied their author's intent and reflected an oppressive social structure.

As a naive undergraduate, I saw postmodernism as the cutting edge of sophisticated thought. The physicist Alan Sokal a few years later made fun of these writers by submitting an article to one of the leading postmodernist journals that argued modern science itself was "socially constructed." The article was published, at which point Sokal revealed the fraud. In a later collected volume, he argued that these French intellectuals wrote in a deliberately obscurantist style to hide the fact that they were talking a lot of nonsense. Jacques Lacan was a psychoanalyst who didn't believe in the possibility of therapy, and whose writings consisted of cryptic aphorisms. One of the pitfalls of being young is that you don't have the judgment to recognize bullshit when you see it, and I was very young at the time.

In later years, I attended an academic conference in Morocco where the participants were steeped in the French intellectual tradition. After I had spoken on a panel, I overheard one of my listeners say to another, "He talks like a journalist." By which he meant that I made clear arguments and didn't partake of the obscurantist language that was prevalent in French intellectual life.

The fascination with postmodernism led me to graduate Cornell early and move to Paris so that I could study with the masters. This was the winter of 1973–74, when the United States and Europe were in the midst of an oil embargo as a result of the Yom Kippur War in the Middle East. On my way I stopped to visit a friend in Oxford at a moment when Prime Minister Edward Heath ordered a shutdown of electricity throughout the UK. A lot of British homes lacked central heating in those days, and all I can remember of the visit was drinking lots of beer and being very cold. I arrived in Paris in January 1974 and soon found an apartment in the 18th arrondissement in Montmartre. That building, at 3, rue Joseph de Maistre, is still there, and the street looks identical to the way it did fifty years ago.

I attended a seminar by Roland Barthes, and lectures at the École Normale Supérieure by Jacques Derrida. Barthes was a very serious writer who had laid part of the groundwork for deconstructionism. Using the terminology of the Swiss linguist Ferdinand de Saussure, he noted that language consists of a series of signifiers that do not necessarily reflect an empirical reality being signified as much as the social structures in which the speaker is embedded. Barthes applied these techniques both to academic writers such as the historian Jules Michelet, as well as to French popular culture. His last book, on photography, *Camera Lucida*, has since become something of a classic meditation on art and society.

I attended Barthes's seminar as part of a Johns Hopkins overseas program. His class seemed to me from the beginning a lot of self-indulgent nonsense. He said he was in the process of writing a dictionary, and each week he would go through a different letter of the alphabet, essentially free-associating from random words: *aimer*, *bébé*, *café*, and so on. Attending this seminar did not seem to be the most productive use of my time, though I did manage to meet an American girl at the class whom I briefly dated.

Derrida was a different matter. He was at that time a rising superstar; his lectures were packed and he was treated as an oracle by his students. Mark Lilla gives an accessible account of his thought in *The Reckless Mind: Intellectuals in Politics*, which I can only summarize here. Derrida built on the foundation laid by Saussure and the anthropologist Claude Lévi-Strauss. The latter attacked the prevailing French narrative of the singular importance of the Rights of Man articulated during the French Revolution as a universal moral framework for politics, and argued that it was just one of any number of possible ways of structuring societies. Saussure argued at a different level that language itself was a socially constructed framework that imposed a structure—often imperfectly understood by the speaker—on perceived reality. Language thus reflected not just the perspective of the speaker but the norms and hierarchy of the surrounding society.

Both of these strands developed in the post-1968 period into a broad critique of the entire Western philosophical tradition, whose underlying concepts—man, nature, the scientific method, empiricism, history, and philosophy itself—were simply social constructs created by a particular society at a particular time to dominate and shape the outside world. This general perspective suited a France that had just fought a vicious colonial war against Algeria's National Liberation Front and then withdrawn from its overseas empire. But Derrida carried this critique further: language itself was not a transparent medium for communicating about and understanding an empirical reality; it always led to contradictions that undermined the self-understanding of the critic. Heidegger used a philosophical vocabulary to deconstruct the Western philosophical tradition, but according to Derrida Heidegger himself was "logocentric" in thinking that his own words and frameworks had stable meanings. This informed Derrida's own communicative style, which was not to proceed with clearly reasoned arguments but was prone to provocations, digressions, and free associations that demonstrated the limitations of language itself.

My time in Paris allowed me not only to listen to Derrida's incomprehensible lectures but also to read through his books, such as the popular *L'écriture et la différence*. I had been accepted with a full scholarship into the graduate program at Yale's Comparative Literature Department, which at that time was the leading center of post-structuralist thought taught by luminaries including Geoffrey Hartman and Paul de Man (another European intellectual later revealed to have had a Nazi past). But by the time I arrived in New Haven in the fall of 1975, I was having serious second thoughts about the wisdom of the course I had chosen.

Post-structuralism and deconstructionism were essentially nihilistic projects built on assertions of the impossibility of reasoned discourse, of inference from empirical evidence, and ultimately of philosophy itself. Truth claims simply masked the assertion of power by a dominant social actor at the expense of groups that were marginalized. The only thing that intellectual activity could hope to accomplish was to deconstruct the ideas of others, to pull away the mask from the powerful and show how their ideas led to self-contradictions or dead ends that escaped their authors' intentions. This approach complemented Michel Foucault's critique of "master narratives," and in particular the narrative of Western modernity centered around modern natural science, liberal politics, and democracy. But these ideas should have been equally destructive of the Marxist framework that informed the agenda of the old left, since Marx shared modernist assumptions about the knowability of history and the value of the scientific method.

Deconstructionism had died out in France by the end of the twentieth century, but these ideas were picked up by Americans and applied to their own situation, which was very much rooted in the country's racial history. Deconstructionism could be aimed at the pieties of the prevailing liberal consensus, which believed in the principles of universal human rights and the rule of law. The very terms in which this narrative was framed could be attacked by postmodernists, as it was actually a project of domination that sought to disguise the continuing reality of the subordination of racial minorities, women, colonized peoples, and later other groups such as gays, lesbians, and transgender people.

What I recognized by the fall of 1975 was that there was a fundamental hypocrisy at the heart of the French postmodernism. The attack on "logocentricity" should be an acid that would eat away at all narratives, including the Marxist ones that informed the Left through the first two-thirds of the twentieth century. But the political sympathies of thinkers such as Derrida and Barthes remained firmly on the left. I remember sitting in the Telluride kitchen with the Bulgarian postmodernist writer Julia Kristeva, who calmly told me that "Stalin had a point."

By this view, oppression of the marginalized by existing power structures was simply another narrative. As postmodernism sank roots in American academia, the marginalized grew more powerful and, by the 2010s, provoked a right-wing backlash. Today, many of Donald Trump's conservative followers would say that "woke ideology" is pervasive and dominant among elites, and that conservatives are the ones being marginalized. It seemed to me that Friedrich Nietzsche and Martin Heidegger, the fathers of modern relativism, were in a way much more honest about the political implications of their thought. Rather than claiming victimhood, Nietzsche embraced the oppressors. Though he didn't use the term, Nietzsche "deconstructed" the Western liberal narrative and argued that it originated in the slave morality propagated by Christianity. This narrative was no more valid than a doctrine that said that the strong should rule the weak. While Nietzsche himself had an ambiguous relationship with anti-semitism, many of his followers would have no problem with it and became supporters of National Socialism when that movement emerged a couple of decades after his death.

These French intellectuals were playing with dangerous ideas at a moment when the Cold War struggle between liberal democracy and Communism was deepening. My father had once dismissed the kind of hyperintellectualized realm I had entered as "intellectual masturbation," and I began to see his point. I wanted to switch to studies that were more directly related to those great ongoing struggles, so I left Yale for the Harvard Government Department the following academic year and never looked back.

12

ON THE EDGE

PART OF MY GENETIC INHERITANCE IS, I BELIEVE, A love of tools. This obviously comes from my paternal grandfather, Keikichi Fukuyama, and his Fukuyama Hardware store in Little Tokyo.

Japan has a deep tradition of carpentry and joinery, and I acquired a lot of Japanese hand tools. Japanese saws, planes, and chisels are like their Western counterparts in most respects, but they all cut on the pull rather than the push stroke. What really sets them apart, however, are the blades. Japanese edge tools build on the tradition of sword makers who supplied Samurai warriors in feudal Japan. The legendary Japanese katana is built up out of thin layers of steel hammered into a single blade, with harder steel in the middle to hold the edge, and softer steel at the sides to give the sword greater structural strength.

The Fukuyama family in LA struggled like everyone else during the Great Depression. But they discovered after my grandfather passed away in 1970 that he had secretly been using the family's money to amass a collection of katanas. He himself came from a farming family, not a Samurai one, so owning the swords must have been a big status symbol for him. My mother, by contrast, came from a Samurai family, and saw their swords confiscated during the American occupation. They are probably now sitting in the closet of a descendant of a wartime GI.

My Uncle Hiroo somehow got hold of my grandfather's sword collection after his death, sold them off, and invested the proceeds in the stock market, where he reportedly lost the entire inheritance. My father never forgave him for this and didn't speak to him before Hiroo passed away in 1987. Only a single sword has come down to me from that collection, and it is a beautiful exemplar of a Japanese blade.

Knowing how to sharpen blades is one of those acquired skills that took me a long time to learn. I had bought a number of high-quality planes when I began my woodworking efforts back in the 1980s—in particular, a German ECE Primus smoothing plane with a beautiful body made of hornbeam, and another Ulmia smoother that had no mechanical adjustment mechanism. On the latter type of plane, as with the Japanese planes, the blade depth has to be set by lightly tapping the back of the plane with a small hammer.

For the first twenty years of my woodworking career, I could never get the hang of hand planing. The plane would chatter, then dig itself into the wood, leaving marks that I would have to sand out. It wasn't until years later that I realized the entire problem lay in sharpening: I simply hadn't sharpened them enough to cut smoothly. You know it's sharp enough when you can pull a piece of paper across it and the paper falls in two pieces with no effort. You also know it's sharp when there are bloodstains on your workbench from accidentally cutting yourself with it.

Sharpening, it turns out, is a separate skill unto itself. Again, the Japanese have the best set of tools for this in the form of waterstones of varying grades. These must be soaked in water, and when used properly will produce a mirror finish on a piece of steel. Once I got the honing technique down, it turned out that planing was a huge joy. I could slide a paper-thin shaving off a piece of wood that was as long as the board itself.

When I was living in Santa Monica in the 1980s, I acquired an antique jointer plane used to flatten the edges of long boards. After cleaning up the rusted blade, I found that it was made by Goldenberg, a company that existed in Alsace prior to the Franco-Prussian War. The plane was therefore over 150 years old. Once I sharpened the blade, it worked perfectly; despite its age, its sole was dead flat and the blade cut beautifully.

My Goldenberg jointer plane, made in Alsace before the Franco-Prussian War

That Alsatian plane I acquired turned out to be one of my most useful tools. In cabinetmaking, if you need to create a wide surface for a tabletop or case, you need to "joint" several narrow boards together and glue them edge to edge. The edges need to be absolutely flat and true, otherwise there will be gaps or cracks between them. If they are properly jointed and you carefully match the grain, a casual observer won't notice that the surface is made of multiple pieces of wood. I used to own a big, heavy power jointer that must have weighed more than a hundred pounds. After I sold all of my big power tools and moved to a small house in California, I found I didn't have enough room in my shop to house one. So I used the 150-year-old jointer plane instead, and found that it was more efficient in creating flat surfaces than the power tool had been. So there's a case where moving from nineteenth- to twentieth-century technology was actually a step backward.

13

CIRCULAR ERROR PROBABLE

WHEN I MADE THE SWITCH FROM COMPARATIVE LITERATURE to political science after the 1974–75 academic year, my original intention was to study political theory with Harvey Mansfield at Harvard as a number of my contemporaries had done. On the advice of an older friend who had become an assistant professor there, I claimed on my application that I wanted to focus on national security studies, since, he told me, there were fewer students wanting to go into that area. So I applied under a false pretext.

Well, not entirely false. I did two of my four qualifying exam fields in ancient and modern political theory with Mansfield, from whom I learned a great deal. Mansfield's lectures were always cryptic and hard to understand, and the challenge of interpreting him inevitably sharpened his students' understanding of the underlying ideas. He wrote widely over a teaching career at Harvard that stretched more than sixty years; if there was a focal point of his scholarship, it lay in his interpretation of Niccolò Machiavelli. Mansfield was one of the few conservative members of the Harvard faculty and drew particular ire for his writings, later in his career, on "manliness." The latter was no simple anti-feminist tract; it grew out of his reading of Machiavelli and the latter's exposition of *virtù*. Mansfield's discussion of *virtù* is one that combatants in today's culture wars should pay attention to, because it defines a different understanding of masculinity from the toxic version being peddled on the right today. Many young men in contemporary societies feel lost because they are given polarized alternatives for gender roles and don't see positive models for behavior. Machiavelli's *virtù* combines courage, self-assertion, the willingness to take risks, and moral probity; while it has traditionally been associated with men, it is a characteristic as well of some of history's greatest female leaders.

I had never taken a political science course up to that point, apart from Bloom's, in political theory. I thought I needed to prepare a bit for my new field, so in the summer before starting at Harvard I began reading a series of books on international relations and nineteenth- and twentieth-century history. This began with Winston Churchill's multi-volume history of the Second World War. For my generation, the story he told was the moral saga that defined the twentieth century: how England slept in the face of rising German power, how feckless politicians sought to negotiate with and appease Hitler, how a terrible war of aggression came anyway, and how an exercise of statesmanship on the part of Churchill rallied his countrymen and allies such as the United States against seemingly overwhelming odds, leading to victory in 1945. After reading Churchill, I went through other classics, including Clausewitz's *On War*, Edward Earle's edited volume *Makers of Modern Strategy*, and Henry Kissinger's book—originally his doctoral dissertation—on Metternich and the

Congress of Vienna. But in the end Churchill's moral tale was so compelling that when I arrived in Cambridge in the fall of 1976 I decided to abandon political philosophy altogether and go into international relations.

The Churchill analogy would later come back to haunt us, when George W. Bush thought he was being a modern-day Churchill in resisting Saddam Hussein.

The world during the late 1970s was in the midst of a newly deepening Cold War. The Soviet Union under Leonid Brezhnev had promoted "bourgeois nationalists" such as Egypt's Nasser and Indonesia's Sukarno during the 1950s and 1960s, but beginning in the late 1970s had shifted, with help from the Cubans and East Germans, to support for more radical self-proclaimed Marxist-Leninist clients in Africa, Central America, and the Middle East. At the same time, Willy Brandt's *Ostpolitik* had brought a thaw to the core of the conflict of the Cold War, a divided Germany, and the United States under Henry Kissinger's stewardship was pursuing détente with Moscow and negotiating a series of strategic arms control accords.

The question at that moment was whether we were in another period like the late 1930s. Were we facing an authoritarian and expansionist great power with naive illusions that we could negotiate with it, or had we foolishly overestimated the power and ambitions of the USSR? The saga of Churchill's resistance to Hitler was a double-edged sword: it could inspire moral courage in the face of overwhelming danger, or it could lead to overestimation of the threat, creating needless and self-defeating conflict. In 1956 Prime Minister Anthony Eden had believed that Nasser was another Hitler who needed to be stopped; the consequent British-French-Israeli intervention in

Suez turned into a debacle and hastened the collapse of the British Empire.

I was definitely in the first camp while in graduate school in the late 1970s. The first article I ever published was one I wrote for *Commentary* magazine in 1979 entitled "The New Soviet Threat." I fell in with a group of hawkish policy advocates, mostly Democrats close to Washington Senator Henry "Scoop" Jackson, including his longtime aide Richard Perle. They believed that any real détente with Moscow was an illusion, and that the United States needed to wake up to the danger of an expansionist Soviet Union. They formed groups such as Team B and the Committee on the Present Danger to warn about complacency in the face of the Soviet threat. The former contested the consensus view of the intelligence community at the time that the Soviet Union was interested in détente and was not an immediate threat to US or European interests. This group would eventually come to be known as neoconservatives.

The most important figure for me back then was Paul Wolfowitz, who was then serving as deputy director of the US Arms Control and Disarmament Agency (ACDA), under an old-timer from Rand, the Swiss-born Fred Iklé. Paul was ten years older than me; both he and his then-wife, Clare Selgin, were, like me, members of the Telluride Association, which was how I met him. As an undergraduate at Cornell he majored in mathematics, but before graduating he met Allan Bloom, who convinced him to shift to political science instead. At the time of the Iraq War, a lot of nonsense was written about Wolfowitz's supposed Straussian roots, and how this had led him to a belief in the necessity of lying as a public official. This was a caricature of Strauss's own views, but also misconstrued Wolfowitz's real intellectual roots. They lay not with Bloom or Strauss but with his mentor at the University of Chicago, Albert Wohlstetter, under whom he wrote a doctoral dissertation on nuclear proliferation in the Middle East.

Wohlstetter became one of my own mentors as well. Wolfowitz had hired me and Steve Sestanovich, my former Telluride roommate and a Russia expert, as interns at the ACDA. Paul's wife, Clare, an anthropologist, was then off doing field research in Suriname, and he offered us a place to stay for the summer that we were in Washington. Paul introduced us to his circle of friends, which included John Lehman (who would go on to be Ronald Reagan's secretary of the navy), Richard Perle (who was to play a key role in advocacy for the Iraq War in 2002–2003), and Edward Luttwak, the defense intellectual who wrote broadly about strategy and Middle Eastern politics. In 1981 I would go on to work for Paul Wolfowitz when he became Secretary of State Alexander Haig's head of Policy Planning.

I met Wohlstetter for the first time at a dinner at the Nanjing Palace, along with Harry Rowen, who was a former president of the Rand Corporation. Harry was not as flamboyant as Albert; rather, he was a thoughtful strategist and policy intellectual. Albert revealed to us at that dinner that he had been approached by a Soviet agent with very large shoes that he suggested might have contained a radio transmitter. Harry Rowen had recently been forced to leave Rand due to Daniel Ellsberg and the Pentagon Papers. Ellsberg had been working on a secret study of the origins of the Vietnam War, which concluded that the government had been lying about the threat and its assessments of the likelihood of military success. Rowen had protected Ellsberg because he believed he was a brilliant analyst, but the latter leaked the study to *The New York Times* in what became an iconic act of whistleblowing.

Albert Wohlstetter had been one of the most famous of the early strategic analysts at Rand. His 1956 bomber basing study argued that the existing nuclear retaliatory force consisted of intermediate-range bombers deployed in Europe, where they were vulnerable to Soviet preemption in a first strike. US nuclear strategy was completely reshaped by this study; the ability to ride out a Soviet preemptive strike became the primary criterion for new nuclear platforms. This led, in the next decade, to the basing of intercontinental ballistic missiles (ICBMs) in hardened silos in the western United States, and to the creation of a fleet of invulnerable missile-carrying submarines. Global stability came to rest thereafter on mutual assured destruction (MAD), in which neither the United States nor the Soviet Union could hope to gain advantage by launching a preemptive first strike. MAD would be challenged repeatedly on both moral and practical grounds, but it has kept the peace successfully in the decades since it was implemented.

Wohlstetter, with his goatee and graying hair, was an unusual character in his own right, who reminded me in certain ways of Bloom. He and his wife, Roberta—another Rand analyst who wrote a classic study of the intelligence failure prior to the attack on Pearl Harbor—lived in a beautiful house up in LA's Laurel Canyon. They had a personal chef and Albert knew the great restaurants on both coasts. He loved eviscerating his political opponents: Marshall Shulman, a Soviet expert at Columbia and a détente advocate, was "such a sweet, silly man."

It was through Albert that I first met a graduate student of his from Afghanistan, Zalmay Khalilzad, who shortly thereafter wrote an article under a pseudonym detailing the Communist takeover of his country, which would lead to the Soviet invasion in December 1979. Zalmay would go on to play big policy roles in the younger Bush's administration as ambassador to both Afghanistan and Iraq, and during the first Trump administration he arguably laid some of the groundwork for the disastrous US withdrawal from Afghanistan in 2021.

Albert at this moment was chief apostle for something that would come to be called the "revolution in military affairs," centering around precision. Bombing precision was measured by something called "circular error probable" (CEP), which was a circle centered on the target within which 50 percent of the bombs were likely to fall. Early in World War II, the British Bomber Command had tried to target German military installations in nighttime raids, but with CEPs of five kilometers or more they had huge difficulties hitting their targets. This led the British, and later the US Eighth Air Force, to shift to the horrendous practice of indiscriminate bombing of civilian targets in hopes that this would break the enemy's will. This inability to hit targets accurately led to the firebombing of Hamburg, Dresden, Tokyo, and other cities in 1944 and 1945, attacks that killed hundreds of thousands of civilians.

By the late 1970s, however, the ability to hit targets from the air had improved dramatically. The US Air Force in the later stages of the Vietnam War had deployed weapons such as the TV-guided Maverick missile, which could accurately take out a bridge in a single shot, while ICBM accuracies were improved to a few tens of meters. According to Wohlstetter, this transformed the nature of warfare: attackers could now hit military targets accurately and avoid the massive collateral damage, with its thousands of civilian casualties.

The problem with the "revolution in military affairs," however, was that while it promised to make conventional warfare less destructive, it also threatened to upend MAD. Accurate ICBMs could be used to target the opposing side's hardened missile silos and take them out in a massive first strike, something known as "counterforce." This would lead to fallout and the radiation poisoning of civilians, but casualties would be in the low millions, and not the hundreds of millions that would result from a full-scale "countervalue" attack on cities. The attacker could not get at the submarine-based missiles but could threaten a countercity blow if the other side did not stand down. MAD would be overturned and nuclear weapons thereby made politically usable once again.

My hawkish friends in this period attacked the ongoing Strategic Arms Limitation Talks (SALT) for not taking adequate account of the possibility of a counterforce strike. In retrospect, the scenario against which they were planning was outlandish: the attacker under these circumstances would almost certainly suffer millions of casualties, and no sane leader would take such a risk. Albert Wohlstetter once argued to me that the USSR had suffered 20 million casualties as the price of victory in World War II, and might be willing to do so again with a "limited" nuclear war. This of course ignored the fact that the war had been imposed on Stalin by Nazi Germany's invasion of the USSR. Stalin was indeed ruthless, but it was hard to see a political purpose that would justify that level of risk-taking. And we know in retrospect that Stalin's successors had a much, much lower risk tolerance than he did.

The issue of the risk tolerance of leaders has once again come to the fore since the beginning of Russia's full-scale invasion of Ukraine. I would go on to write my doctoral dissertation on Soviet threats to intervene in the Middle East. Looking at six Arab-Israeli crises up through the 1973 Yom Kippur War, I concluded that in each case Moscow had threatened to intervene militarily, but only after the peak of the crisis had passed and the likelihood of making good on their threats was diminished. Vladimir Putin unfortunately has rendered this thesis completely invalid. He has taken risks that the old Soviet leadership was never willing to do, intervening in Georgia, sending troops to Syria and Venezuela, and launching a massive invasion of Ukraine. Putin has frequently threatened to play his ultimate trump card of nuclear escalation since the beginning of the full-scale war, threats that were sufficient to deter the Biden administration from providing more powerful weapons to Ukraine. Putin's risk tolerance is not unlimited, however; the Ukrainians have repeatedly crossed supposed "red lines" of his during the war, with no sign that Russia was willing to use nuclear weapons. And he would certainly not risk a nuclear first strike unless he saw his own empire collapsing.

14

UNREALISTIC

IF YOU TAKE A UNIVERSITY-LEVEL COURSE IN INTERNATIONAL relations theory these days, you will be taught that there are several frameworks for understanding how international politics works that go under headings such as liberalism, realism, neorealism, constructivism, and the like. "Realism" has gotten a fresh look since the beginning of Russia's full-scale invasion of Ukraine in February 2022, in particular through the writing and advocacy of the University of Chicago professor John Mearsheimer and the work of places such as the Quincy Institute. Mearsheimer's form of realism is seen as a counterpoint to the democratic messianism said to have been infecting American foreign policy over the years, in which the United States has allegedly tried to reshape the world in its own liberal democratic image through the use of force. The Ukraine conflict by this light is seen not as a struggle between an emerging democracy and an authoritarian great power, with America standing on the side of democracy, but rather as a clash of national interests where the United States itself played a role in provoking the conflict.

I don't want to argue the specific case of Ukraine at this

point, but rather to reflect on my understanding of realism and how it has affected my views of American foreign policy over the years. As I tried to explain in my 2006 book, *America at the Crossroads*, I consider myself a "realistic Wilsonian," which means I believe that liberal values and power shape the country's role in the world, while being realistic both about the extent to which the United States can prioritize democracy and the means by which such a goal could be achieved.

There are in fact two types of realism, the first of which I would label a "realism of means," and the second a "realism of ends." I have known John Mearsheimer since we were both graduate students, and he has built his career around the elaboration of the latter understanding of politics.

The realism of ends fits the whole of international politics into a theoretical framework under which all states are said to pursue national interest defined in terms of power and security. They may dress up this drive in the elevated language of democracy or human rights, but ultimately all states seek the same thing, the maximization of national power. This type of realism sees the international system as a whole as anarchic, with no overall sovereign or common set of rules to regulate state behavior. Hence one state's search for security inevitably threatens the security of others; peace emerges only because there is a balance of power that deters any one state from overreaching. States in the international system are like billiard balls; you can't look inside them to see their goals; what you can know is their mass, velocity, and position on the table.

The realism of ends has always struck me as a hopelessly reductionist and oversimplified way of describing state behavior. In that respect it is a bit like the rational utility maximizer model of neoclassical economics that reduces all behavior to the pursuit of material gain. Of course power and relative position matter in the international system, but nation-states are complex actors whose behavior is intimately connected to the domestic politics taking place inside them. "National interest" is not a fixed characteristic, any more than is "utility" in economic theory. National interest can be defined in a variety of ways, often reflecting a country's governing values. Moreover, emotions arising out of pride and *thymos* can take hold of populations as well as individuals, and lead to self-destructive behavior. Democratic states with internal checks and balances will inevitably behave differently than authoritarian ones lacking such institutional structures.

In particular, the United States has always seen the promotion of democracy and a liberal form of government as part of its national identity and something that would benefit the rest of mankind. It has never pursued these goals single-mindedly, and has consequently opened itself up to charges of hypocrisy. But it has often mobilized its own people to sacrifice and international involvement on the basis of the need to support a liberal and democratic world order. If the United States were simply trying to maximize its power, it wouldn't act this way. In this respect, I think the realism of ends gets the world profoundly wrong.

The kind of realism to which I have subscribed from the beginning is a realism of means. Even if our national purpose is to assure the survival of democracy and human rights abroad, this cannot be done without power. That power can be economic, social, or cultural, but at the end of the day what really matters is military power. Authoritarian leaders like Adolf Hitler or Vladimir Putin can only be stopped by military means.

This is why I have always been skeptical of international

law. International lawyers often talk as if ratifying an international convention will have a decisive effect on actual state behavior, regardless of the nature of that state's regime. But law without the power to enforce is typically ineffectual. Russia may have violated countless human rights laws and norms in its invasion of Ukraine, but the only thing that will bring an end to these violations is defeat on the battlefield.

From the perspective of the realism of means, there are a host of shibboleths about international relations that are simply false. It is sometimes argued that political solutions are always superior to military ones. A variant of this observation holds that war never solves anything, or that all wars end through negotiation.

None of these accord with actual history, however. The dichotomy between force and diplomacy is a false one. Diplomacy needs to be backed by force or the threat of force; diplomatic solutions will endure only if it is in the clear self-interest of the parties to stop fighting. It is not the case that all wars end by negotiation: many conclude with a decisive victory of one side over the other. Consider the federal government's victory over the Confederacy in the American Civil War, or the Allied defeat of Germany and Japan in the Second World War. The only things that were negotiated in these cases were the terms of surrender. You may not favor the victorious side, but this kind of settlement tends to be much more durable than those in which evenly matched rivals come to a diplomatic settlement. Those tend to collapse the moment the power balance shifts. Henry Kissinger shared a Nobel Prize for negotiating the end to the Vietnam War, but the accord was violated the moment the Vietnamese Communists felt they could defeat South Vietnam on the battlefield.

The realism of means, however, does not dictate the particular ends that a state may seek. During the first Gulf War in 1991, the United States intervened to uphold the principle of state sovereignty; it was seeking neither the broad goal of bringing democracy to the Persian Gulf, nor the narrower one of access to oil. It obviously used violent means to achieve this goal. But the realism of means is not necessarily a formula for militarism or aggression; rather, it often implies that a great power must show restraint in its pursuit of objectives, however defined.

The fundamental problem with the second Gulf War, the US invasion of Iraq in March 2003, was that the Bush administration's goals had broadened to regime change. Its immediate objective was the elimination of Iraq's supposed stockpile of weapons of mass destruction (WMDs), and policymakers believed this could not be done as long as Saddam Hussein remained in power. What the authors of this war did not understand was that the United States did not have the power to create a stable, friendly regime in Saddam's place.

The invasion of Iraq was driven by genuine concern over that country's alleged possession of WMDs. The conspiracy theories that say the Bush administration knew there were no WMDs and invaded for other motives are simply wrong. When no such weapons were found, the administration turned to democracy promotion to justify what was becoming a bloody and costly debacle. George Bush's second inaugural address presented a soaring vision of a world transformed by universal democracy, and laid the geopolitical problems of the Middle East at the doorstep of Arab dictatorships.

Needless to say, the US administration struggled mightily to stabilize post-Saddam Iraq, and did not remotely have the ability to bring about this more expansive end. Realistic

Wilsonianism might have accepted a democratic Middle East as a very long-term objective, but would have abjured the use of raw military power to bring this about in the short run.

Part of the reason that many would-be realists critique the idealist strand of US foreign policy flows from the rhetoric that came out of the administration of George W. Bush to justify the Iraq War. This rhetoric was a profound mistake: it led people around the world to believe that military force would be the primary instrument for spreading democracy and that American aims in that regard were universal and unlimited.

Obviously, realistic Wilsonianism presents an alternative to this caricature of American policy. For all of the hypocrisy that has characterized US foreign policy over the years, the country's rhetorical commitment to a liberal international order and support for democracy around the world has provided a principled basis for continuing involvement in international affairs. It has softened the harsh politics that would flow from a superpower truly committed to a realism of ends, and has focused US attention on abuses of power abroad that are actually susceptible to US influence. It has also facilitated democratic transitions in places like Chile, the Philippines, and South Korea.

With the advent of the second Trump administration, we are entering a new phase in American history, with a president who abhors the term "democracy" and has prioritized the crudest form of material self-interest—both national and personal—as the guiding principle of his foreign policy. It constitutes a return to the nineteenth century, in which great powers sought to expand their territorial extent and divided the world into spheres of influence. This may appear to be a form of realism, but it is not.

15

THE END OF HISTORY

I COMPOSED MY ESSAY "THE END OF HISTORY?" SITTING in my in-laws' house in Las Vegas in the winter of 1988–89. I was preparing for a lecture at the University of Chicago organized by Allan Bloom and Nathan Tarcov at the Committee on Social Thought. Bloom was habitually pessimistic about the ability of Western liberal democracies to defend themselves, and the overall rubric of the lecture series was "The Decline of the West." I told Bloom I was happy to participate, but that I would have a more optimistic take on what was going on in the world. He said that was fine, and I gave my talk a year before the fall of the Berlin Wall. Owen Harries, an Australian former ambassador, was the new editor of a small magazine founded by Irving Kristol called *The National Interest*. He had lunch with me at the Beverly Hills Hotel that winter and asked whether I had anything to contribute. I told him about my upcoming lecture, and he promised to publish the written version, which came out in the summer of 1989. By this time I had already left my job at Rand and moved to Washington to serve as a deputy director of the State Department's Policy Planning

Staff under Secretary of State James Baker and his Policy Planning chief, Dennis Ross.

The phrase "the end of history" was not my invention; rather, it was central to the thought of the philosopher Georg Wilhelm Friedrich Hegel. As noted earlier, Hegel was the first explicitly historicist philosopher; that is, a philosopher who argued that human thought and institutions were not fixed but evolved over historical time, and that the "truth" of a particular assertion needed to be judged in relation to the historical era in which it was articulated. We may not believe in the legitimacy of monarchy or slavery today, but there were certainly times in the past when many people did support such ideas. The fact that we believe in democracy and equal rights today is testimony to the reality of "History" in Hegel's sense.

The idea that human societies evolve over time took root only in modern times. Both Plato and Aristotle argued that there was a cycle of regimes that succeeded one another, but that this led to cyclical change that simply reproduced previous forms of government in succession. The idea that history was progressive, that it had a beginning point in primitive societies but moved toward more complex and advanced ones, was adumbrated by Jean-Jacques Rousseau in his *Discourse on the Origin of Inequality* under the heading of "perfectibility." His description of "man in the state of nature" was not simply a thought exercise, as it was for Thomas Hobbes, but an actual effort to describe human behavior that drew on what Europeans at that time knew about non-Western societies. Europeans were aware of the existence of other sophisticated societies, such as those of Islam and China, but the opening up of the New World suggested societies differed in what we would today call their level of development. Hegel simply systematized the idea of History and provided an intellectual structure for understanding what drove that evolution.

The notion that societies evolve over historical time in a progressive fashion is tacitly accepted by almost everyone today, whether they self-consciously understand that fact or not. The idea of a Hegelian history is embedded in our words "development" and "modernization." Organizations such as the former US Agency for International Development (USAID) and the International Bank for Reconstruction and Development (i.e., the World Bank) were both dedicated not to simply helping poor countries become rich, but to helping them create modern institutions that make life more secure and predictable.

The most important intellectual to accept and then modify Hegel's concept of history was Karl Marx. Hegel argued that history had evolved into the modern liberal state in the wake of the French Revolution. Marx criticized Hegel's understanding of the end of history and argued that the true end of the human development story would be a Communist utopia. This would come only after the working class rose up and displaced the bourgeoisie, establishing a dictatorship of the proletariat. At the Marxist end of history, the alienation brought on by the capitalist division of labor would be abolished and human beings would be able, as Marx said in *The German Ideology*, "to hunt in the morning, fish in the afternoon, rear cattle in the evening, criticize after dinner."

My particular understanding of Hegel did not come directly from Hegel but from Hegel's twentieth-century interpreter, the Russian-French philosopher Alexandre Kojève, whose debate with Leo Strauss I recounted earlier. Kojève taught an extremely influential seminar on Hegel's *Phenomenology of Spirit* in Paris in the late 1930s that was attended by many luminaries who would go on to become major figures in the French postwar intellectual firmament: Georges Bataille, Raymond Queneau, Jacques Lacan, André Breton, Éric Weil, Maurice Merleau-Ponty, and Raymond Aron. As noted earlier, he had an extended dialogue with Leo Strauss on philosophy and tyranny, and got to know Allan Bloom as well. Kojève's lectures were later transcribed and published as *Introduction to the Reading of Hegel*.

Kojève of course accepted Hegel's historicism, but he made historical progress revolve around a critical human characteristic: the desire for recognition. Human beings do not simply desire material resources such as food, clothing, and shelter; they also crave the respect or recognition of other human beings. This struggle for recognition results in bloody battles at the beginning of history as individuals seek dominance; those who achieve it becomes masters, while the losers become slaves. But neither the master nor the slave finds his desire for recognition fully satisfied: the slave for obvious reasons, but the master as well because he is recognized not by another master but by a slave.

In Kojève's account, human beings are unique insofar as they seek recognition for their willingness to risk their lives in a bloody battle. Other creatures in nature are instinctively programmed to preserve their own lives or the lives of their offspring; only human beings are willing to risk their biological lives for the sake of recognition alone, as opposed to, say, the material spoils that come as a result of victory in war.

In this respect, Kojève's human being is similar to that of his predecessor Immanuel Kant. Kant believed that what makes human beings distinctive is their possession of moral will, an ability to choose right or wrong that is ultimately not subject to the laws of physics. Human beings therefore have to be treated as ends in themselves rather than as a means to other ends. But in Kojève's interpretation of Hegel, masters cannot achieve the satisfaction of recognition until they realize that this will come only with the equal and mutual recognition of fellow citizens. My particular gloss on Kojève/Hegel was that this could only come about in a modern liberal state, where the equal and mutual recognition of all citizens was guaranteed by a rule of law that granted them basic rights. The liberal state was legitimate and stable not necessarily because it distributed material rewards equally, but because it provided equal recognition and thus satisfied the thymotic side of human striving.

In his *Introduction to the Reading of Hegel*, Kojève playfully asserted that history ended in 1806 at the Battle of Jena-Auerstedt, where Napoléon defeated the Prussian monarchy. The idea that history ended that year, prior to all of the huge political upheavals that followed in the two subsequent centuries—Italian and German unification; the American Civil War; the colonization and later decolonization of much of the non-European world; two World Wars; the Holocaust; revolutions in Russia, China, Iran, and elsewhere—is on the face of it much more absurd than an assertion that it ended in 1989 or 1991 when Communism collapsed. But what Kojève meant by this is summed up in the following passage from his lectures on Hegel:

> What has happened since then [i.e., the Battle of Jena] has been nothing but an extension in space of the universal

> revolutionary force actualized in France by Robespierre-Napoleon. From the genuinely historical perspective, the two World Wars with their train of small and large revolutions have only had the effect of bringing the backward civilizations of the outlying provinces into line with the (really or virtually) most advanced European historical stages . . . It might even be said that, from a certain point of view, the United States has already reached the final stage of Marxist "communism," since all the members of a "classless society" can, for all practical purposes, acquire whatever they please, whenever they please, without having to work for it any more than they are inclined to do.

With the defeat of the Prussian monarchy in 1806, Napoléon brought to the core of old Europe the Code Napoléon, the modern legal framework coming out of the French Revolution. The latter established the underlying principles of a modern liberal order, namely, the two principles of liberty and equality, or the equality of liberty. Obviously, these principles were nowhere truly implemented. As Napoléon was advancing in central Europe, for example, the French colonial authorities were putting down a slave revolt led by Toussaint Louverture in Haiti; colonization of Algeria and Vietnam were still decades in the future. But Kojève's point was that once the idea of universal freedom got out, it was only a matter of time before those principles became accepted and practiced around the world. Toussaint himself had started his uprising, for example, under the banner of the Rights of Man and of the Citizen that had recently been declared in Paris. So there were rearguard actions to defend the old order everywhere, but in the end they would not stop the march of the idea of liberty, or of the equality of liberty.

The implication of this understanding of Kojève/Hegel was that no amount of "stuff happening" out in the real world of global politics could by itself falsify the notion that history had ended, whether in 1789, 1806, or 1989. The actual diffusion and spread of the ideas of liberty and equality have been very uneven both temporally and geographically since the French Revolution. The real question had to be understood not just in terms of the flow of day-to-day events around the world, but on the level of ideas: Was there an alternative set of principles upon which a different society could be based that were fundamentally at odds with those of the French Revolution? And were there societies built around those ideas that looked like they were sustainable, and would satisfy the wishes of their inhabitants better than existing liberal democracies built around those principles?

These would be the grounds for a serious refutation of Kojève's assertion that history had ended.

The original essay "The End of History?" appeared in *The National Interest* in the summer of 1989, when I had started working as a deputy director of the State Department's Policy Planning Staff under my old colleague Dennis Ross. The Berlin Wall came down a few months later, on November 9, and set in motion a series of events that would lead to the dissolution of the former Soviet Union two years later. The emergence of a Europe "whole and free," as George H. W. Bush put it, was the greatest geopolitical event of my lifetime, and vindicated the historical direction I had pointed to in the article.

Today's ideological landscape is obviously far more fragmented than it was thirty-five years ago. There is today far more consensus on the democratic side of liberal democracy than there is on the liberal part. While there are obviously huge remaining social inequalities in many societies, few try to assert that there are reasons why a certain subgroup of people has an intrinsic right to rule over others. The PRC is a dictatorship, but the Chinese Communist Party claims a right to rule because it believes it represents the people: it is the *People's* Republic of China. Ethno- and religious nationalism have been on the rise in recent decades. Most of these groups represent rearguard efforts to protect perceived privileges, rather than assertions of the inherent inequality of groups. In the United States, we've seen the ugly return of earlier forms of racism and misogyny. But groups taking such positions do not seem poised to systematically overturn the Declaration of Independence's assertion that "all men are created equal."

What has been under much more sustained attack in recent years is the liberal part of liberal democracy; that is, the idea that governments should be constrained in their powers by a rule of law and constitutional checks on state power. Much of the democratic backsliding we've seen over the past decade has in fact been driven by groups claiming to represent "the people," whose democratic legitimacy gives them the right to dismantle the constraints imposed by liberal restrictions on state power. Hence Viktor Orbán's claim to be presiding over an "illiberal democracy."

Support for liberalism, as opposed to democracy, has always been more fragmented and episodic. The reason for this, as I explained in *Liberalism and Its Discontents*, is that one of its important justifications is a pragmatic one concerning the management of political diversity, rather than any deep commitment to the liberal principle. Support for liberal constraints on state power is often derived from the experience of authoritarian government and the wars and privation that the latter often entail. So seventy years of relative peace and prosperity can lead to a broad forgetting of what illiberal rule can bring.

Liberalism also raises the problem of the Last Man, which is not a contingent but an intrinsic issue buried in the heart of the doctrine. This is an issue to which I will return.

16

TRUST

AFTER ALL THE NOISE SURROUNDING THE PUBLICATION of *The End of History and the Last Man* settled down, my publisher at Free Press, Erwin Glikes, called me to ask what I'd like to write next. Erwin was a conservative who had shepherded me through my first book; he was controversial for having published Charles Murray's *The Bell Curve* on IQ and race and wanted to provide an outlet for different voices. But he gave me lots of freedom to write what I wanted and advised me, among other things, that I didn't necessarily have to answer the question I was asked during TV interviews. This was good advice; the veteran TV and radio interviewer Larry King once fell asleep as he interviewed me on his late-night program. He couldn't have cared less what I said.

It had never occurred to me that I'd be able to write a second book on any topic I wanted, and I realized what an incredible opportunity that was. Most young academics climbing the greasy pole have to worry about tenure from the moment they take their first job, and getting tenure means falling in line with the prevailing methodological and other orthodoxies in their particular sub-sub-discipline. This is why their first books are usually full of unreadable jargon; the tenure candidate is writing for an incredibly narrow group of specialists who will determine whether he or she will win the big prize of lifetime employment. If they succeed in getting tenure, they can (as Harvey Mansfield put it) "raise the Jolly Roger" and write anything they want, but by then they've been socialized into the habits of their particular discipline and are unlikely to break out of its confines.

Though I eventually wound up being a professor, in those years I hadn't wanted to climb the academic ladder and hoped to do public policy instead. But now that *The End of History* was out I could write freely on other subjects. I told Erwin that I wanted to write something on the relationship between culture and economics. My father had gotten his PhD in sociology at the University of Chicago and left me his library of sociology classics: Max Weber, Émile Durkheim, Karl Mannheim, Ferdinand Tönnies, Karl Marx, Ernst Troeltsch, and many other works of classical social theory. While he was alive I resisted reading them, but by the time he passed away in 1995 I realized that I really wanted to learn this literature. As with my first book, I spent several months simply reading everything I could on the subject of culture and economics. Leo Strauss was a critic of Weber and social science more generally, which saddled his followers with an aversion to social theory. This had left a huge gap in my education.

The reason I picked this topic was a bit accidental. I remember having read in graduate school that during the Second World War the British Special Air Service had captured an entire German radar station in France and brought it back to England to reverse-engineer it. They were at the time behind in radar technology, but they realized as they took it apart that it had been machined to tolerances that could not be matched by British manufacturers. This little anecdote stuck with me, and I wondered why it was that some countries were good at certain activities, such as making precision machinery, but not at others.

On the general topic of culture and economics, there was of course a huge literature sparked by Max Weber's *Protestant Ethic and the Spirit of Capitalism*. But it didn't seem to me that I could add much to this debate. It was in the course of reading through the older literature that I came upon the concept of social capital. This term had been used in the 1950s by the urbanologist Jane Jacobs in her book *The Death and Life of Great American Cities* to describe the unplanned social networks that kept order in American cities. The concept was picked up by the sociologist James S. Coleman as an explanatory factor in economic life. While I was in the midst of this research, Robert Putnam published, in the *Journal of Democracy*, his essay "Bowling Alone," where he argued that America's traditional propensity for voluntary organizations had deteriorated over the previous fifty years, and that levels of trust and social capital were now much lower. It struck me that the concept of social capital was an important one that had never been adequately explored in either sociology or economics, so that became the focus of my second book.

Social capital, as I defined the term, was the informal ability of people to work together, underpinned by certain virtues or habits such as openness, honesty, and a propensity for keeping commitments. It was possible to get people to work together through formal mechanisms such as labor contracts, hierarchical organizations, and the like, but social capital properly referred to what amounted to a cultural propensity to cooperate. A society where people were generally honest and reliable would not see the need for lawyers and thick contracts guarding against every possible form of cheating, but could rather economize on these transaction costs. Alexis de Tocqueville famously argued in *Democracy in America* that Americans were very good at forming voluntary organizations, and that the latter facilitated democracy and political participation. This stood in sharp contrast to his native France, where he observed that you could not find "ten people to work together on a common task."

I wanted to name the new book "Social Capital" in a throwback to Marx's three-volume work, or else possibly "Art of Association" as a nod to Tocqueville. My editor at Free Press, Peter Dougherty, urged me, however, to use the title "Trust" instead. He said that the word "trust" had universally positive associations and would be especially popular among business readers. I balked a little at this, since in my view trust was a by-product of social capital and not its cause. But my editor was absolutely right about this, and the book went on to sell well in many countries around the world—especially in those such as South Korea that I had labeled "low-trust" societies. I know of no part of the world that thinks it has enough trust, or that it isn't facing a crisis of trust.

Indeed, looking closely at the phenomenon of trust led me to some important insights. Trust is necessary for any society to function, but the "radius of trust" varies from one society to another. People are biologically wired to trust other family members and close friends, but societies differ greatly in the degree to which they trust people outside their immediate circle of friends and family. As I read into the literature on East Asia, it became clear that China and Japan differed markedly in this regard. China was similar to the Southern Italy that Edward Banfield had characterized as low-trust and characterized by "amoral familism": it was very difficult for people there to trust people outside the family, and larger civic institutions were missing. Putnam himself would pick up on this insight in his book on Italy, *Making Democracy Work*, which confirmed empirically the huge social differences that existed between Northern Italy, where broad social trust existed, and the south, where it did not. Similarly in China, there was a cultural emphasis on obligations to family members that was not nearly as powerful in neighboring Japan. In China, an entrepreneur who started a business was obligated to turn it over to his son, and the company would often fail if the son was incompetent. Japan had a more flexible system where strangers could be brought in to run the family business. You had your daughter marry a competent husband and then turned the business over to him. That son-in-law would take the daughter's family name, something that didn't happen in China. In Chinese cultures such as those of Taiwan and Hong Kong, family businesses dominated and remained relatively small, while Japan made a transition to large-scale corporate organizations much earlier in its modernization drive.

A "familistic" society is one in which trust largely exists within kin groups but doesn't extend beyond the family. Once you understand the concept, you begin to see it manifest in many domains. I had spent relatively little time in Latin America at the time I wrote *Trust*, but in the subsequent two decades I went there a lot. I came to realize that many Latin American countries were similar to Southern Italy: their economies were dominated by a small number of family businesses, which often failed to expand because of a reluctance to bring strangers into the organization. The family is a basic unit of social solidarity, but it can also be an obstacle to broadening the radius of trust, with both economic and political implications.

I tried to fit the theories in *Trust* into a Tocquevillian framework when I wrote it in the mid-1990s. Tocqueville argued in *The Old Regime and the Revolution* that France's low degree of trust stemmed from the centralizing tendencies of the French monarchy, which were simply carried forward into modern France by the Revolution. Citizens came to be dependent on the government for everything, and never developed the habits of spontaneous social cooperation that existed in the United States. I saw this as a good explanation for the problems of Eastern Europe and the former Soviet Union, where dictatorial Communist parties had centralized power and actively discouraged any form of spontaneous social organization outside their control. This dependence on the state hindered the emergence of a vigorous civil society and a democratic political culture long after Communism collapsed.

As time went on, however, I came to realize that the state crowding out civil society was only part of the problem. Colombia at that time was falling into a massive crisis due to the rise of narco-trafficking gangs such as the one headed in Medellín by Pablo Escobar, and a long-standing insurgency by the Fuerzas Armadas Revolucionarias de Colombia, or FARC. This led in turn to the formation of paramilitary organizations hired by ranchers and businessmen to protect their property. There was, needless to say, little trust in a society where middle-class people were regularly kidnapped and held for ransom by one or another of the criminal organizations plaguing the country.

The problem in Colombia was not an excessively strong state, but rather an excessively weak or absent one. The central government in Bogotá simply did not have the capacity to defend a rule of law throughout the country, and as a consequence people who could afford it bought their own protection. There was no legitimate monopoly of force in the country: the paramilitaries sponsored by wealthy elites turned from protection of their masters to extortion and drug dealing. This problem was addressed only with the election as president in 2002 of Álvaro Uribe, who, with help from the United States under Plan Colombia, began building up the military and national police. Uribe did not solve the problem of the drug trade, but he did succeed, with help from Colombia's civil society, in sharply reducing the level of violence in the country.

A similar story could be told in Southern Italy. The Mafia emerged in Sicily due to the absence of a strong state, and not because of an excessively powerful one. Before Italian unification and independence in the late nineteenth century, the Kingdom of the Two Sicilies was ruled by a distant power in Spain that never succeeded in establishing anything like a consistent rule of law. As that regime weakened in the nineteenth and early twentieth centuries, individuals began to hire mafiosi as private protectors of their property. Just as in Colombia, these private agents moved from protection to extortion, and then to drug dealing, human trafficking, prostitution, and other lucrative criminal activities.

The state, in other words, played a big role in the formation of social trust. If it was too strong and pervasive, as in ancien régime France or the former USSR, it could undermine trust, but if it was too weak, as in Colombia or Southern Italy, it could spawn a dystopian form of civil society ruled by predatory gangs. The legitimate monopoly of force represented by the state was critical in creating trust and allowing it to flourish.

A lot has changed since I wrote *Trust* in the mid-1990s. In the tradition of Tocqueville, my chapter on the United States portrayed the country as a high-trust society. Civil society and spontaneous organization flourished there, as did a vigorous private sector driven by entrepreneurs who didn't have to wait on the government to take initiative. I took part in the debate spawned by Putnam's *Bowling Alone*, and argued that civil society remained strong in the United States, but that its form was changing. His book was published just as the internet was being privatized and made available to everyone, and social connectivity was shifting from in-person to online.

In 2025, it is no longer possible to describe the United States as a high-trust society. The American propensity for spontaneous horizontal organization has not diminished; in that respect, the technological opportunities offered by the internet and social media have led to an explosion of social interconnectedness. The real problem is twofold. The groups into which American civil society has organized itself have become highly politicized and polarized, and levels of generalized social trust have plummeted. People within the red and blue teams trust one another, but express extraordinary levels of distrust, often verging on outright hatred, for their opponents. The second decade of the twenty-first century saw the rise of a populist movement led by Donald Trump that trafficked in distrust. Populism can be defined in a number of ways, but one of the most important is the belief that established organizations—the media, political parties, universities, big businesses—are being secretly manipulated by elites who want to use them for their own purposes. Populism is built around an explicit call to distrust existing institutions and to use political power to undermine them. This has led to an inability to agree on simple factual information, such as who won the 2020 presidential election or whether vaccines are safe.

The second way that trust in America has declined concerns trust in public institutions, i.e., the government. Distrust of the state has always been one of the core elements of American political culture, something traditionally shared on both the right and the left. But this distrust has evolved to truly pathological levels in the second decade of the century, particularly on the right. Americans are being told that their government is being actively turned against them, falsifying election outcomes, lying about statistics, engaging in politicized prosecutions, manipulating the public health system, and conspiring to change the country's demographics by opening the southern border to illegal immigrants. Certain politicians such as Robert F. Kennedy Jr. have risen to prominence by trafficking in the most outlandish conspiracy theories, such as the assertion that the moon landings were faked or that Covid was bioengineered to target specific ethnic groups.

As I argued back in the 1990s, trust is critical to the efficient working of both the economy and the political system. It is hard to see how the economy will prosper if consumers are picking products according to their partisan affiliations, or how the state will function if people have lost faith in the criminal justice system. A new edition of *Trust* would need to have a very different chapter on the United States as a low-trust society.

17

SEYMOUR MARTIN LIPSET

I NEVER TOOK A POLITICAL SCIENCE COURSE AS AN undergraduate, except for a couple of political theory classes. As a graduate student in the Harvard Government Department, I began to do so, but these were limited to international relations. To this day I have never formally studied American politics. I liked to think that everything I knew about this topic, I learned from Seymour Martin Lipset long after my formal education was finished.

Marty Lipset was one of the twentieth century's greatest social scientists, having been president of both the American Political Science Association and the American Sociological Association. I only encountered him in the 1990s, after he had left Stanford to teach at George Mason University in northern Virginia. In the early part of that decade I had returned to being a consultant at the Rand Corporation while writing my first two books, and received a query as to whether I was interested in a position in the new Institute of Public Policy at George Mason. At this point I wanted an academic position. I had had two tours in government, and decided I was not meant to be a bureaucrat. At the same time, I had come to understand that my real ability lay in writing books. That is what academics, by happy coincidence, are paid to do. Bloom once said that he couldn't imagine a better life than being a tenured professor, and I could now see the truth in that. So I accepted George Mason's offer, which came with a named chair and academic tenure. I managed to short-circuit the entire painful process of being an assistant professor up for tenure review.

It turned out that Marty Lipset had played a role in the invitation. In this period, the "Institute" was housed in a couple of double-wide trailers in Fairfax, Virginia, and in one of those trailers sat the great Seymour Martin Lipset. He had just published his book *American Exceptionalism: A Double-Edged Sword*, and had built a graduate course around a comparison between American political institutions and those of other developed democracies. He wanted a co-teacher, a job I was happy to do, and this course became my introduction to American politics.

Marty was a comparativist who regularly warned his students that a person "who knows only one country knows no countries." Since his early book *Political Man*, he had focused on the ways in which the United States differed systematically from almost every other modern democracy in the world. The United States, unlike most European democracies, had never had a powerful socialist party. But the deepest source of difference lay in long-standing distrust by many Americans of government, or the state, which Marty argued originated in their revolt against monarchical authority and the British Parliament.

There was a time not too long ago when Republicans such as Newt Gingrich celebrated American exceptionalism, and argued that the United States had qualities that were not shared by any of the world's other democracies. Marty's view was different: America was both exceptionally good in certain respects, and also exceptionally bad in ways that were connected to its virtues. Thus Americans' distrust of the state and of authority in general led them to be less dependent on the government, and more entrepreneurial and innovative than people in other countries. Apple Computer in the early days of personal computers produced a famous commercial that urged viewers to "think different" about technology, and break away from stodgy older firms like IBM. From then until the present age of artificial intelligence, American firms have been more innovative than their counterparts in Europe and Asia. But this willingness to defy authority also meant that Americans were prone to defy legitimate authority as well. Crime rates tended to rise and fall in tandem across developed democracies, but those in the United States were always higher than those of other democracies.

According to Marty, hostility to and distrust of the state has been one of the most foundational characteristics of American political culture. Americans assume that a state exists, and that the main political problem is how to limit its power to preserve individual freedom. The United States was born in a revolution against the authority of the British Crown and Parliament, and the struggle against tyrannical authority is baked into the consciousness of every subsequent American. This is true on both the right, where vows to dismantle the "deep state" have become a staple of conservative thought, as well as on the left, where there is widespread belief that corporate power has captured a national security state.

Distrust of state authority led to a constitutional system with many more checks and balances than in other democracies. It has consequently always been harder to pass major legislation in the United States than in other democracies, which was why, according to Marty, the American welfare state came later and was always less extensive than social safety nets in other democracies. In contrast to virtually every other rich country, the United States had no nationally mandated health insurance system until the passage of Obama's Affordable Care Act in 2010, and the Republicans then spent much of the next decade trying to repeal it. In other democracies, people see universal access to health insurance as a basic right; in America, many feel it is a dangerous form of socialism.

Marty could be quite oblivious to his immediate personal circumstances. The senior faculty at the Institute had periodic informal meetings known as the Popcorn Club at the house of a colleague, Don Kash, and Marty's chair would be surrounded by a layer of popcorn kernels that had somehow failed to make it into his mouth. His eyesight was poor and he didn't drive, so as in the case of Allan Bloom I found myself chauffeuring him all over town. He was dyslexic as a young man, and his lack of language facility caused him to focus on Anglophone countries such as Britain and Canada for much of his comparative work. One result was that he became one of North America's foremost experts on Canada. He was an incredible fount of knowledge, not just about American institutions but about global politics, and knew personally virtually every important social scientist of his generation. While his political preferences tended to be center-right, he was good friends with figures on the left, including the feminist Betty Friedan.

Marty passed away in 2006 in a way many of us fear. He suffered a stroke that took away his ability to speak or otherwise communicate, yet lived another five years bound to his bed at home. I would visit him and talk, not knowing whether there was a Marty Lipset still there inside his body who could hear me, but was not able to acknowledge my presence.

We are now entering a very different period in American history. America's sense of its own exceptionalism was symbolized by the Masonic pyramid with the all-seeing eye on the dollar bill, with its accompanying inscription *Novus ordo seclorum*, or "New order of the ages." The American republic saw itself from the beginning as an inspiration for other countries, whose institutions and democracy were things that the rest of the world aspired to. Donald Trump is the first American president to explicitly deny that America is exceptional. When an interviewer described Vladimir Putin to him as a killer, he responded, "We've got a lot of killers. You think our country's so innocent?" He has no idealistic illusions about what the United States represents in the world; to him, all countries, including America, are simply pursuing their self-interest without regard to broader principles, as he himself does.

The death of America's sense of its own exceptionalism may not be an entirely bad thing. During the lead-up to the Iraq War in 2003, I was struck by the way many supporters of the war believed that the United States had the right to invade other countries because of its good intentions as the world's leading democracy. They would be the first to denounce any other country that acted in a similar fashion. It was American exceptionalism that gave it leave to act as it wished.

As Marty Lipset explained over the course of his career, American exceptionalism was a double-edged sword.

18

WOMEN AND THE GREAT DISRUPTION

CONSERVATIVES ARE ALWAYS DECRYING MORAL DECAY, and such decay indeed happens. Both the United States and Britain experienced an increase in social dysfunction from the early nineteenth century on. This was particularly evident in terms of alcoholism, which was epidemic in the United States in the 1820s and 1830s. But the next fifty years saw a variety of religious revival movements that remoralized much of society, peaking during the Victorian era in Britain and in a corresponding rise of Puritanism in the United States. The perceived social disorder created by an urbanizing society and massive immigration gave way to a backlash that included the passage of the Eighteenth Amendment banning the sale of alcoholic beverages, and the Johnson-Reed Act of 1924 severely limiting immigration.

During the 1980s and early 1990s, there was great pessimism concerning society's moral order. Beginning in the late 1960s, there were significant increases in crime rates, especially in large cities; divorce rates increased, as did rates of births out of wedlock and single-parent families. Birth rates were also beginning to fall, and many conservatives attributed these phenomena to the loss of religious belief and spreading secularization.

This was the background to my least-read book, *The Great Disruption: Human Nature and the Reconstitution of Social Order*, which was published in 1999. In many ways, the research I did for this book taught me more about modern societies than did any other project I had embarked on up to that point. In particular, it made me understand the central importance of gender in shaping norms and social outcomes.

There is a general conceit that the rise of feminism in the 1960s was an autonomous moral event, in which people around the world began to acknowledge the essential equality of men and women, much as they have come to accept equality of the races. Today, some on the far right believe it is a consequence of "woke ideology." But as I explained in *The Great Disruption*, feminism was not simply a cultural awakening; it was driven by deeper socioeconomic forces that explained its timing and extent. Beginning sometime in the late 1950s and 1960s, the nature of work began to change as developed economies transitioned from industrial to postindustrial ones, or what we call an "information" society. Machines became ubiquitous as substitutes for human labor for both men and women. Machines also became smarter as computers proliferated and spread. As economies shifted from manufacturing to services, jobs increasingly involved sitting behind a computer screen rather than lifting heavy objects off the factory floor, or digging ditches with hand shovels. In this kind of a world, women had a much more natural place. Especially at younger ages, they are more self-disciplined and less inclined to take foolish risks than men.

The consequence was that women began to move in massive numbers into the paid labor force beginning in the late 1960s. Women began to get much better educations, and found that they could outperform similarly situated men in a variety of fields. In addition, the birth control pill was invented in the early 1960s, de-linking (at least in theory) sex from reproduction. Since women tend to be attracted to men who are older and of higher status than themselves, the ratio of available women to men in dating and marriage markets rose as the post–World War II baby boom increased the birth rate. This gave men more bargaining power and encouraged more casual relationships. This was the permissive condition for the sexual revolution, which took place more or less simultaneously with the rise of feminism.

These technological and economic changes then had huge downstream consequences for families, children, birth rates, and gender relations. Women began to displace men in workplaces. Importantly, they were no longer dependent on men to support them and their children. Social institutions such as the "shotgun marriage" had arisen because in earlier societies, women had limited opportunities to earn independent incomes. Fathers therefore needed to force the young men who impregnated their daughters to stick with them over their lifetimes. Once female economic independence became possible, the shotgun marriage faded away. Families began to break down as women realized that they did not have to remain trapped in oppressive patriarchal households.

Crime rates began to rise in this period as well. This was due in part to changes in family structure. Men felt enabled to leave their wives or girlfriends more readily in search of other partners, leaving the women to raise children on their own. In poor neighborhoods, children often had to raise themselves because their mothers worked and their fathers were absent. This had bad effects on educational outcomes and socialization, especially of young men. There were exogenous factors operating as well: the rise of the cocaine trade and heroin led to an epidemic of drug addiction and created huge incentives for illegal behavior. Violent crime, which is typically committed by young men, also rose because there were simply more males coming of age in the late 1960s after the baby boom of the 1950s.

At the same time, women started voting in greater numbers in this period, which on the whole was good for the spread of liberal democracy. Female policy preferences differ markedly from male choices: they tend to support social programs such as childcare and education, while men often push for defense spending and are more willing to risk conflict. This was one of the factors encouraging the spread of liberal democracy in this period.

So the Great Disruption that many Americans experienced as long-term social decline was driven by specific socioeconomic forces including the birth control pill, computers, mechanization, and the rise of services. The argument I tried to make back in 1999 was that societies would over time adapt to these changes. Decline was not a one-way street because human beings are highly social creatures who do not like to live without norms or rules. Remoralization would take place, not necessarily as a result of a religious revival, but because humans by nature are creatures who liked to create rules for themselves.

This is largely borne out in social developments that have been taking place in the quarter century since then. Crime rates began coming down in the early 2000s; New York among other cities regained control of its neighborhoods, and complaints shifted from urban decay to excessive gentrification. Divorce rates fell as well, and the percentage of single-parent families stopped its seemingly inexorable rise. Latchkey children came under the supervision of helicopter parents.

This occurred, however, only for a limited part of American society. The restoration of social norms took place primarily among upper-middle-class professionals. The Great Disruption's social pathologies had taken root early on primarily among African Americans. They affected working-class whites as well, but spread among that group on a much larger scale in the 1990s and the early twenty-first century. In place of crack cocaine and heroin, working-class whites were hit with an opioid and methamphetamine epidemic, leading to the current phenomenon of "deaths of despair."

The Great Disruption also had longer-term political and demographic consequences. A large part of the white working class that had traditionally been a core constituency of the Democratic Party's coalition began to desert it for the Republicans, beginning with Ronald Reagan's two elections. This trend continued into the twenty-first century, and was particularly true for young men. The 2024 election saw Democrats making strong appeals to women on issues such as abortion, but they had less of a program to sell to men, including Black and Hispanic working-class males who felt disrespected in a world that constantly celebrated female achievement. The Republicans, meanwhile, were celebrating various forms of toxic masculinity.

The Great Disruption also lies at the heart of what is increasingly viewed as a global crisis of depopulation. Birth rates have fallen everywhere, but particularly in the rich world. Such societies include Italy, Spain, Japan, Singapore, Taiwan, and South Korea, the last of which has a total fertility rate at present hovering just below 0.8, far below the replacement rate of 2.2.

In my view, the basic driver of low fertility is related to female education and employment. A stay-at-home mother is essentially an uncompensated worker; with female incomes and job opportunities rising, it made sense for women to enter the paid labor force and to outsource the raising of children to nannies. Having more children thus represents both opportunity costs and higher expenses, expenses not just for childcare but for housing, education, and the like. Virtually everywhere in the rich world, more young women are receiving higher educations than men, and would therefore have better lifetime earning potential.

The collapse of fertility was consequently most severe in countries where women were given higher educations but faced legacy patriarchal cultures that don't support female work outside of the home. Many educated women react to this by choosing to have fewer children, or putting off marriage and childbearing altogether. The only countries that have succeeded in raising their fertility rates—slightly—are those in Scandinavia that have provided generous state-supported childcare allowances. The combination of educated women, patriarchal cultures, and low levels of government childcare likely explains the extraordinarily low fertility rates in the developed countries of East Asia. Loss of religious values has nothing to do with it—South Korea with its disastrously low birth rates remains a country with one of the largest active Christian populations in the world.

All of this points to several implications that were not clear to me when I wrote *The Great Disruption* a quarter century ago. I was right in arguing that normative decline is not something that necessarily takes place in an autonomous cultural sphere; rather, it is often driven by powerful socioeconomic and technological forces. With regard to the kinds of normative changes that have hit the developed world in recent decades, the decline of traditional religiosity is more likely to have been a symptom rather than a cause. And societies do respond by renorming themselves; human beings do not like the condition Durkheim called "anomie" and will respond by creating new rules.

But normative change always moves more slowly than technological change, and the latter does not necessarily stop or slow down periodically to allow societies to catch up. I've always been skeptical of the view that the pace of technological change is continually speeding up. The economic historian Robert Gordon argued that the period from 1870 to 1970 saw far more technological change than the decades after that period, with the advent of innovations such as internal combustion engines, use of gas and oil, airplanes, electricity, indoor plumbing, computers, vaccines, and the like. But whatever the rate, change is relentless, and the cumulative impact of the shift to an information economy has been enormous for politics and society. The one thing that hasn't accelerated is the pace of normative change, which continues to operate in generational increments.

19

HUMAN NATURE

TO ME, IT SEEMS OBVIOUS THAT THERE IS SUCH A THING as human nature—that is, a set of faculties, behaviors, and constraints that characterize the human species as a whole and differentiate humans from chimpanzees and gorillas, not to speak of goats and earthworms.

Human nature has been critical in the development of Western political philosophy, and hence of politics. Socrates in *The Republic* posed the question of what is true of humans "by nature," and what is merely customary. Customs are subject to change and can be deliberately shaped by societies, while human nature has a permanence that gives it a priority with respect to human ends. To take one example, human languages vary across cultures, but the faculty for language is common to all cultures, Greek or barbarian, and the ability to use language has been closely connected to human reason and social organization.

Thomas Hobbes, one of the founders of modern liberalism, began his book *Leviathan* with a comprehensive catalog of human passions, which could be understood as his understanding of human nature. Hobbes famously asserted that there were no natural moral rules, and that the war of "every man against every man" led to a state of violence and insecurity that made life "nasty, poor, brutish, and short." This situation was in turn the product of two fundamental human passions, the desire for "gain" or the resources beloved by economists, and also a desire for "glory"—that is, for the estimation of one's worth by other people as superior. Though Hobbes did not use Plato's terminology of *thymos*, that is what he was talking about, and in particular, the dangers of *megalothymia*, the desire to be recognized as superior to other people.

Hobbes's account of human nature then leads directly to his understanding of politics. The violence of the state of nature fuels the strongest natural passion, which is the fear of violent death. This becomes the grounds for his argument that the "first right of nature" is the right to preserve one's own life. In the anarchic state of nature, human beings could not avoid threatening one another's lives. The Leviathan, or state, was necessary to create a social compact by which each person gave up a little natural liberty for the sake of preserving his or her life. The desire for security from the fear of violent death was a stronger passion than, say, the desire for a pleasant summer vacation or for a forty-hour workweek, and therefore had priority in the hierarchy of basic rights. Hobbes's "right to life" was the progenitor of Thomas Jefferson's right to "life, liberty, and the pursuit of happiness" asserted in the US Declaration of Independence. This was the "natural law" tradition running from Aristotle through Thomas Aquinas up through Hobbes, Locke, and the American Founding Fathers.

Hobbes is rightly understood to be one of the founders of modern liberalism, even though his Leviathan was hardly what we would today describe as a liberal state. It was he who first argued that rights inhere in individuals, who voluntarily agree on a social contract. Most of the big political controversies of subsequent centuries revolved around alternative understandings of human nature, and therefore of the kinds of political systems that needed to be derived from them.

For example, John Locke, who exercised enormous influence over the American Founding Fathers, had a softer view of human nature that encompassed a natural proclivity to acquire property, and to make it more productive. Private property emerged when human labor was combined with the "almost worthless things of nature," and became the basis for market exchange and thus economic growth. Jean-Jacques Rousseau disagreed explicitly with Hobbes, arguing that "natural man" was not violent or greedy, but rather a timid, solitary creature who had within himself the capacity for happiness. The lust for resources and glory that Hobbes described came about only when early humans came together in societies and began to compare themselves to one another. Society rather than human nature was thus the source of competition, violence, and feelings of envy. Human happiness could be restored only by recovery of the authentic "natural man" that lay behind the customs and pressures created by an external "society."

Although they differed among themselves, these early modern thinkers' theories of human nature laid the grounds for modern liberalism. Hobbes, Locke, and Rousseau all posited that the state of nature consisted of isolated individuals pursuing their own ends, and that human societies emerged only later as people agreed to cooperate as a means of achieving their individual ends. The only form of human society that was natural was the family, where sexual desire drove men and women into mutual dependence. This view remains at the core of modern neoclassical economics: the fundamental assumption is that human beings are rational utility maximizers who come to understand that they can increase their individual well-being by working with one another. This becomes the basis for Mancur Olson's widely used theory of collective action, where social cooperation is primarily driven by individual incentives. In John Locke's account of marriage and reproduction, the family is not grounded in emotional ties arising from human nature, but is rather a voluntary union based on a rational calculation of long-term self-interest.

Primordial individualism is thus an assumption about human nature that lies at the heart of modern liberalism, both political and economic. In this respect these thinkers broke with Aristotle's view that man is a "political animal" by nature, who can only experience a flourishing life in a city. The individualist assumption would be directly attacked by thinkers on the left, beginning with Karl Marx, who held that human beings were by nature social creatures who sought collective rather than individual ends. Liberal individualism was seen to be a historically contingent phenomenon that appeared with the growth of modern capitalism, but which gravely distorted understandings of human happiness.

But liberalism's individualist assumptions were attacked not just from the left, but from the right as well. The great English legal theorist Henry Maine already in the mid-nineteenth century noted that what was known about early societies contradicted the individualist assumption: there was never a time, as far as the historical record showed, when human societies did not exist. There was no period of history characterized by the isolated individuals of Hobbes, Locke, and Rousseau. Following Charles Darwin and evolutionary theory, it further became clear by the twentieth century that mankind's nonhuman progenitors also lived in social groups of varying complexity. What distinguished the left- and right-wing critics of liberal individualism concerned the type of social group to which human beings were naturally attracted. For Marx and his followers on the left, it was large social classes such as the bourgeoisie and proletariat, or, at the end of Marxist history, a Communist state. For people on the right, from Johann Gottfried Herder to Oswald Spengler to contemporary national conservatives, it was cultural groups from tribes to nations to civilizations. The specific beliefs underlying different cultures were variable, but there was a natural human proclivity to produce culture, and to live within a closed cultural horizon.

The differing assumptions about human nature represented by Hobbes and Rousseau have big implications for contemporary arguments over environmentalism and, indeed, the nature of human happiness. Hobbes presented a secular version of the Christian doctrine of original sin: human beings were by nature greedy, fearful, violent, and vain; it was only by coming together under a social contract that these natural passions could be kept under control. Rousseau, by contrast, reversed the valence of inside and outside: human beings were naturally good; it was only their entry into society that corrupted them and made them unhappy. The Rousseauian assumption is today shared by many anthropologists and environmentalists, who tend to believe that indigenous societies are more peaceful and environmentally protective than people in modern industrial ones.

For the last couple of centuries, many people in liberal Western societies have shared Rousseau's assumption about the "natural goodness of man." This is true insofar as they value inner authenticity, and believe that it is the pressures of "society" that suppress that authenticity and deny them the happiness they would naturally enjoy. In a Hobbesian world, growing up entails acceptance of the fact that one cannot do whatever one wants, and that a successful life requires conformity with social rules. In a Rousseauian world, by contrast, the inner self is constantly seeking liberation from stifling social constraints, whether the latter are enforced by a state or simply by social custom.

The discovery of DNA and the genetic code in the 1960s provided a heretofore missing biological account of inherited physical and behavioral traits. Given this, and the ubiquity of belief in human nature, it may seem surprising that there has been a huge pushback against the very concept, and outright denials on the part of serious thinkers that human nature exists.

There were a number of reasons for this skepticism. In the first place, as knowledge of genetics increased, it became clear that our genetic inheritance interacts with our social and physical environment in very complex ways. Human beings are not robotically programmed to behave in determinate ways like certain animal species. Faculties may be rooted in the human genome, but their development can be extended, enhanced, or, conversely, constrained by how an individual is brought up and interacts with society. Geneticists discovered that certain genes are expressed only in response to specific environmental signals. It was therefore sometimes hard to say what core human capacities exist "by nature."

We know a lot more today about human nature than we did in the eighteenth or nineteenth century, not just as a result of advances in biology but also because of research coming from archaeology, comparative anthropology, and indeed primatology. From the vantage point of the present, it is safe to say that the early modern liberal narrative about the state of nature was wrong in several respects. I presented evidence for this in the first volume of my *Political Order* series. Human beings are social by nature, but their sociability takes certain characteristic forms. The biologist William Hamilton's theory of inclusive fitness posits that human beings—indeed, not just human beings but most sexually reproducing species—are altruistic in proportion to the number of genes they share with relatives. They are also strongly inclined toward reciprocal altruism; that is, the exchange of favors or benefits with close colleagues. This means that the most prevalent form of social life lies in community with a small circle of friends and family, which in turn means that patrimonialism—that is, rule by friends and family—is deeply natural. By contrast, the kind of impersonal authority required by a modern state where officials are chosen on the basis of merit does not come naturally to political actors. For this reason, "repatrimonialization" is a constant threat in modern political systems. We see this today as Donald Trump seeks to undermine a merit-based bureaucracy, relying instead on a close circle of trusted friends and family.

But this kind of small-scale sociability does not exhaust the human capacity for community. Human beings may have individual interests, but they are also by nature norm-following animals who are loath to deviate from the rules established by their peers. The willingness of individuals to comply with rules set by large hierarchies has been the basis for state authority ever since the invention of the first states some six to eight thousand years ago. The rule-following proclivity explains why policemen are willing to carry out manifestly unjust orders against fellow citizens, or why millions of soldiers have gone to their deaths in battle. Thomas Hobbes's belief in rational self-interest led him to argue that soldiers rationally ought to desert their posts rather than risk their lives fighting enemies, and yet obedience has been much more characteristic of military organizations over the centuries than desertion.

More recent data also suggests that Hobbes may have been closer to the truth than Rousseau with regard to propensities of early peoples toward violence. The latter's assumption about the "natural goodness of man" is unfortunately contradicted by a fair amount of empirical evidence: many hunter-gatherer societies have higher murder rates than contemporary American cities, and evidence of bloody warfare extends backward in the archaeological record as far as we can see. Humans are social creatures by nature, but their sociability is often driven by the need to organize violence. Environmental stewardship appears to stem more from a lack of technological capacity than from intention. The world's megafauna were largely wiped out following the entry of modern humans into those regions where they existed.

So human nature exists, and is a powerful force shaping politics and our ideas of rights. Why then does it meet such resistance?

The reasons are moral and political, and often are by-products of misunderstandings of human nature. Over the years, the question of what is biological and what is environmental has been the source of enormous political controversy. Broadly speaking, conservatives have tended to take the side of biology, while progressives have argued that behavior is strongly conditioned by the surrounding environment—that is, behavior is "socially constructed." Over the centuries, conservatives have believed that nations were rooted in common race and ancestry; that there was a racial hierarchy that legitimated slavery at home and Europe's colonial domination of much of the rest of the world; and that women did not have the mental capacity or emotional stability to enter the workplace, vote, or become political leaders.

It is safe to say that these and other political uses of biology have been losing propositions. Some of the changes in understanding were simply the result of flawed empirical scientific research. A famous case from the 1920s involved the work of the anthropologist Franz Boas, one of the founders of modern cultural anthropology. Following the publication of Darwin's *On the Origin of Species*, a school of "scientific racism" emerged, arguing that, among other things, the world's races differed in average intelligence, with white northern Europeans coming out on top. In the 1920s conservatives argued in favor of restrictions to immigration on the grounds that the groups coming into the United States during the great wave of the late nineteenth and early twentieth centuries—Italians, Jews, Poles, and other Eastern Europeans—were less intelligent than the then-dominant ethnicity in the States. This argument was based on a measurement of head sizes done by the US Army as soldiers were being inducted to fight in Europe. Boas did a follow-up study that showed that the head sizes of immigrant children converged with those of northern Europeans when fed an American diet. Later studies of the so-called Flynn effect showed that average IQs were going up over time for population groups all over the world as a result of better diet and nutrition.

Controversies over the role of biology reemerged big-time with the rise of feminism in the 1960s. Many feminists were strongly on the social construction side, arguing that apparent male-female differences in either behavior or social outcomes were due exclusively to the way that girls were brought up in contrast to boys. Women had to be liberated from the social conventions that made it hard, for example, for them to enter a variety of professions, from driving trucks and piloting airplanes to serving in the police and military.

But while biological arguments about what girls and women could or could not do were steadily debunked, there remained a core set of male-female differences that could not be overcome. Men and women obviously differ with regard to physical characteristics, in ways that go beyond the fact that they have different reproductive organs. Height, upper-body strength, longevity, and other features may be normally distributed for both sexes, and there will be individuals in the tails of the distributions that will outperform the vast majority of members of the other sex. But the medians of those distributions differ. So while any individual woman may be stronger or taller than any individual man, the characteristics of the sexes will not be the same in the aggregate. This is why male and female sports remain segregated to this day.

These differences very likely extend to psychological characteristics as well. In the 1980s evolutionary psychologists began to argue that male and female reproductive strategies differed, not just among human beings but among many sexually reproducing species. Men tended to be more promiscuous than women because that was their optimal strategy for getting their genes into the next generation; women by contrast needed stable homes in which to raise their children to adulthood. Adolescent women are also less inclined to risk-taking, which is why the vast majority of crimes are committed by young men in cultures all over the world.

The idea that *any* behavioral trait could be explained biologically did not sit well with many feminists. The sociobiologist Edward O. Wilson, who had argued that gender differences were rooted in biology, had a pitcher of water dumped on his head at a conference by an activist shouting "You're all wet!"

There is another, even more fundamental reason why progressive liberals resist granting significance to human biology: it represents an intolerable limitation of human autonomy.

At the core of modern liberalism is an assertion of the equality of human dignity, based on a posited universal human capacity for choice. Human beings may differ in terms of intelligence, strength, skin color, and gender, but all are deemed moral agents who have the ability and the right to make choices about their own lives—rights to speech, belief, association, and the like. Protecting that autonomy has been regarded as the moral core of a liberal society. In early modern Europe, autonomy was understood as the right to make choices within a preexisting moral framework established by religious tradition. Freedom of religious belief was therefore one of the key values protected by rights, as in the US First Amendment.

Over time, however, the sphere of autonomy expanded relentlessly to include the ability not just to make choices within a moral framework defined by an existing religious tradition, but also to choose one's framework and even make up moral rules for oneself.

This is nowhere more evident than in the sphere of sexuality, gender, and family life. Many countries have legalized abortion, which is typically framed as a way of protecting the autonomy of women to control their own bodies. But the final frontier in the denial of the significance of biology is the contemporary transgender movement. Transgender activists, supported by a good part of the medical establishment, assert that gender is wholly unrelated to biological sex; that is, to one's XY chromosomes. Rather, it is a matter of individual choice, much as one might choose a new name or a place to live. They don't want to be told that their genetic endowment will have powerful effects on their gender identity.

The notion that there is a strong underlying relationship between biological sex and gender identity became one of those verboten ideas in certain liberal circles during the 2010s and 2020s, a prohibition that has been rigorously enforced by transgender activists. The idea is not a very plausible one, however. It doesn't make sense to think that people were choosing their gender identities over the centuries as a result of social pressure alone: the rootedness of human beings in their biological sex is a necessary precondition for reproduction and family life to take place. It would undermine Darwin's theory of natural selection, not to mention his whole theory of sexual selection, which goes down the drain under these conditions. There have always been a small number of individuals who were unhappy with their gender identities, and in a liberal society their choices need to be respected.

But one cannot build a political right around a characteristic that may or may not be natural, and is shared by only a small minority of human beings.

Technology promises to take away the limitations of human nature, but this is a false promise. I believe that we are moving into dangerous territory here. Human beings are not disembodied wills floating in space that can choose to land in any shape or form they choose. Our human experience, and therefore the ends and goods that we seek, have been deeply shaped by our physical bodies and the strengths and limitations that they entail.

This is why I wrote my 2002 book, *Our Posthuman Future: Consequences of the Biotechnology Revolution*. Human beings have been using technology to enhance their physical and mental faculties continuously throughout history. We are faster and stronger, see better, travel farther, live longer, through technologies from eyeglasses to automobiles to vaccines. Biomedical technology can already shape behavior and outcomes through surgery, drugs, and other interventions. Many Silicon Valley oligarchs have been throwing money at technologies for life extension.

The emergence of genetic engineering made possible by technologies such as CRISPR-Cas9 promises much more fundamental changes to those underlying faculties that may one day alter our understanding of political rights. Do we really want to be able to freely change our underlying natures, to make human beings more or less aggressive, more or less compassionate, more intelligent, or more servile? We may not like the proclivity for risk-taking and violence, but what unanticipated consequences may flow from an effort to breed it out of the human race? And who is it that will be exercising the power to decide these issues, decisions that will affect not just subjects in the present generation but all of their descendants? Will these powers be exercised by wealthy elites, who can then give their descendants a leg up in social competition in centuries to come?

A further issue is that while autonomy is a human good, it is not the sole human good that trumps all other ends that people choose. Part of the human experience lies in coming to terms with limitations, both those that apply to us as individuals and those that are true of human beings as a species. Indeed, those limitations are what link us in communities. Many people deliberately want to live within a religious or cultural tradition that binds them in communities, even as it restricts their freedom of individual choice.

As the Latin poet Horace said, "You can throw nature out with a pitchfork, but it will always come running back." We will never become gods, and may learn that lesson only as we approach our two hundredth birthdays with the diminished faculties of five-year-olds.

20

DIZZY WITH SUCCESS

MY MAIN CONCERN ABOUT LAUNCHING AN INVASION of Iraq was not the illegality or immorality of intervention. Force had been used for good purposes in the Second World War, and in the 1991 Gulf War. The United States had succeeded beyond all expectations in deposing the Taliban regime in Afghanistan in the fall of 2001. I assumed that the military side of regime change could be done quickly and effectively. The problem that was most worrisome to me was what would happen on the day after the regime's downfall, and how the United States would manage the rebuilding of a new Iraq.

A lot of my academic interest in the 1990s centered on developing countries and the difficulties that outside powers such as the United States had had in bringing peace and stability to them. One of my mentors in this period was Stephen Hosmer at Rand. He was a counterinsurgency expert who had started his Rand career during the Vietnam War when Rand had a Saigon office. He was not opposed to the use of American power in developing world conflicts, but understood very well the limits of that power. According to him, the problem was twofold: First, neither the United States nor the "international community" had the mechanisms or the cultural knowledge to develop functioning institutions in poor countries. Second, the American public had little patience for nation-building, especially when it involved prolonged insurgencies. According to Steve, the United States was constantly entering these conflicts but tiring of them after a few years, something that was true in the Philippines after the Spanish-American War in 1898, Nicaragua in the 1930s, Vietnam in the 1960s, El Salvador and Nicaragua again in the 1980s. Americans were supportive of the use of military force at first, but grew impatient later as the recipient countries remained unstable and failed to develop economically or politically. The United States would then walk away from the project it started, in Hosmer's view shamefully abandoning those local allies it had vowed to support. Many of these places ended up in much worse shape than if an intervention had never happened in the first place. Afghanistan is only the latest instance of this pattern.

This is exactly what worried me about the prospective invasion of Iraq. It was not apparent that the Bush administration had clear plans for how to govern the country once the Ba'athist regime had fallen; there was vague talk about bringing exiles like Ahmad Chalabi back but nothing about how that would be seen as either legitimate or effective.

Proponents of military action against Iraq had become, to use Stalin's phrase, "dizzy with success," and thought that the democratic momentum of 1989–91 would carry through to the Middle East of the early 2000s. Senior officials in the Bush administration, including Paul Wolfowitz, his deputy Scooter Libby, Condi Rice, Steve Hadley, and many others had last been in office in the elder Bush's administration when Communism fell. They had not been around during the frustrating nation-building interventions in the Balkans and Latin America during the 1990s. The idea that American troops would be met with cheering crowds of well-wishers reflected the experience of Eastern Europe in the late 1980s, where there was indeed broad-based popular happiness over the fall of Communism and regime change. This was what encouraged them to believe that Iraq would see a relatively easy and peaceful transition to democracy.

The Middle East was, as it turned out, a very different place. While many Arabs didn't like the dictators they were living under, they also had a very jaundiced view of the United States and American power. The United States, after all, was the chief supporter and armorer of Israel, and protected the authoritarian regimes in the Persian Gulf despite protestations of support for democracy and human rights.

The Bush administration argued that culture did not constitute an insuperable barrier to the spread of liberal democracy to the Muslim world. But it was a factor: in contrast to democratizing Eastern Europe, many majority-Muslim countries hosted Islamist parties that were often strongly illiberal. Even when they failed to come to power, the threat that radical Islamism posed acted as a spur to authoritarian government in response. This logic would play out in Egypt in the wake of the Arab Spring, where General Sisi, with the support of many middle-class Egyptians, staged a coup to prevent rule by the Muslim Brotherhood.

The reality that unfolded subsequently in Iraq was much worse than I feared. The administration had made virtually no preparations for an extended occupation of Iraq; Defense

Secretary Donald Rumsfeld, it turned out, believed that the United States could turn Iraq over to Ahmad Chalabi and withdraw from the country before the end of 2003. Exiles such as Chalabi were opportunistic charlatans, and the original mistake of invading was compounded by huge misjudgments, including the decision by the viceroy Jerry Bremer to disband the Iraqi army, a choice made before he even landed in Baghdad.

As Steve Hosmer had predicted, the American public grew tired of the war after a few years of deepening conflict. While Bush was reelected in 2004, he was succeeded by Barack Obama, who had opposed the war from the start.

The Iraq War was to have huge negative consequences for the United States, the full extent of which would become apparent only in the succeeding two decades. The rise of Donald Trump and his isolationist followers was stimulated by the failure of the Iraq intervention and the belief that the nation had been manipulated into supporting it by elites. The Iraq War marked a sharp break between the United States and its European allies, a break that has only gotten worse in recent years. Some of the war's architects continue to defend the war by arguing that the world is better off with Saddam Hussein gone, but this ignores the huge price that was paid to achieve this goal. The war was, in the first place, a huge waste of human lives and incubator of human suffering, first and foremost for the Iraqi people that the invasion was supposed to benefit. Rather than becoming a beacon of democracy in the Middle East, Iraq has turned into a corrupt and chaotic satellite of Iran, despite the oil revenues it receives. American credibility was severely undermined; to this day, many on the left and in the Arab world believe that the Bush administration knew there were no WMDs in the country and invaded out of shadowy ulterior motives. This cynicism about the origins of the war extends to a large part of the American public. Donald Trump's rise after 2016 was powered in part by his opposition to America's "forever wars." Between the Bush administration and the present, the Republican Party has moved from strong support for an internationalist foreign policy to its isolationist roots that oppose American involvement in the world as a whole. Donald Trump has simply articulated openly what many Americans had come to feel, that American foreign policy was manipulated by elites for their own benefit.

21

ON CHANGING YOUR MIND

GETTING OLDER AND MORE ESTABLISHED HAS BOTH advantages and disadvantages. The disadvantages are obvious. Most people's worldviews—their attitudes toward politics, whether they are liberal or conservative, their posture toward money—are shaped by their life experiences as they are growing up, up until the age of thirty or so. Thereafter, their views become more rigid and are hard to shake; to the extent they change, they remain directionally stable but more extreme. People like my father, who grew up during the Great Depression, tend to be very risk averse and careful about their personal finances; those growing up in the *Bonfire of the Vanities* 1980s are more flamboyant and spendthrift.

This is one of the reasons why I have always been skeptical about life extension technologies, and the basic drive in biomedicine to help people live longer. There is a good evolutionary reason why human beings die, summed up in the joke that the field of economics advances one funeral at a time.

Human societies would never evolve if there were not generational turnover; a world in which people routinely lived to be 150 or 200 would be a nightmare. I once had a debate on this subject with the science editor of a libertarian magazine who gushed about the possibilities for life extension. I responded that I was not looking forward to a world where he would be able to spout the same dumb libertarian views a hundred years from now.

At the same time, there are certain advantages to getting older that point in the opposite direction: you can more easily change your mind. A person's worldview is shaped not only by the large events occurring as he or she is growing up—wars, financial crises, social unrest, the broader culture—but also by their circle of friends who shape the way these events are interpreted and experienced. Human beings are unfortunately not the rational individuals of classic Enlightenment liberal theory who take in empirical data and infer from them theories of how the world works; rather, they start with outcomes they prefer and use their impressive cognitive abilities to find evidence to support those outcomes. And where do those preferred outcomes come from? Human beings are intensely social creatures who take their cues from the circle of people around them. Breaking with their friends and colleagues is an intensely uncomfortable thing to do, and people will maintain absurd positions in order to avoid putting themselves on the outs with their in-group. Republicans have put themselves through incredible contortions in recent years to justify their support for Donald Trump. Some of them are doing this cynically to hold on to power, but others actually come to believe the contradictory things they are saying, something explainable only in social psychological terms.

This is where a certain kind of security about one's social status can be helpful. By the early 2000s, I was teaching as a tenured professor at the Johns Hopkins School of Advanced International Studies (SAIS) and had a few well-regarded books under my belt. My in-group up to that point had been the circle of neoconservative intellectuals who wrote for Irving Kristol's *The National Interest*, or *Commentary* magazine in its heyday under Norman Podhoretz. *Commentary* had published my first article in 1979; I wrote for it frequently in subsequent years and did a regular series of op-eds for *The Wall Street Journal* under its editorial page editor Bob Bartley.

Saddam Hussein's Iraq had become a central issue in American foreign policy during the 1990s. George H. W. Bush liberated Kuwait in 1991 after it was occupied by the Iraqis, but prudently stopped short of going on to Baghdad and deposing Saddam Hussein. The latter was insufficiently chastened by his battlefield defeat; he played a cat-and-mouse game under UN sanctions and continued to pursue various weapons of mass destruction programs in this period. UNSCOM, the United Nations inspection agency that revealed these activities, was expelled from Iraq in 1998. When the weapons inspectors returned under new authority as UNMOVIC in 2002, they assumed that Saddam Hussein was lying and covering up continuing WMD efforts, an assumption that laid the groundwork of the debacle of the invasion. Saddam also continued a system of totalitarian repression at home, killing and torturing critics and rivals, using poison gas against the Kurds, and defiantly rejecting the Oslo peace process being pursued by the Clinton administration at the time.

However, in this bygone era Americans did not understand how well they were doing. The period from the fall of the Berlin Wall in 1989 until the subprime crisis of 2008 represented the peak of American global hegemony: Soviet Communism and the Warsaw Pact had collapsed and the countries of Eastern Europe were democratizing and seeking entry into the European Union and NATO; China under Deng Xiaoping had recommitted itself to modernization under a market economy; and the United States was dominant in every aspect of power: economic, political, cultural, and military. The US defense budget in this period was larger than that of all the other major powers combined. There were wars in the Balkans, genocides in Rwanda and Darfur, and other sources of instability outside Europe and Asia, but the major debate in US foreign policy at that time was over what was called the "responsibility to protect"; that is, a positive duty on the part of the international community to intervene on behalf of human rights and democracy around the world.

It was against this backdrop that my old friend from graduate school Bill Kristol, along with Robert Kagan, established in 1997 the Project for a New American Century. They argued that the geopolitical landscape was not benign, that Americans, like the British in the 1930s, were being hopelessly complacent, and that the country needed to massively increase defense spending in response. The organization's first target was China, and it sought to build consensus in favor of a China containment strategy. My feeling at the time was that Kristol's project was looking for enemies, motivated less by the existence of a real foreign threat than by the Republican

Party's need for an issue with which to beat the Democrats in the next election.

Al-Qaeda attacked the United States on September 11, 2001, and destroyed New York's Twin Towers. That morning I was in my office at SAIS in downtown Washington. My colleague Karl Jackson, an expert on Southeast Asia, came in and said that I should turn on the TV. The first tower had been hit, and we saw the second plane crash into the other one soon thereafter. Out the window of our building on Massachusetts Avenue, we could see smoke rising from the Pentagon across the river, and we all realized our lives would be very different from then on. Karl said, "Somebody is going to pay for this."

All of a sudden it did appear that there were serious foreign threats in the world and that the United States had been asleep at the switch. I had just started my professorship at SAIS that month, and remember the extraordinary discussions that took place that fall about how the world had suddenly changed. Previous terror attacks had always had some specific political goal in mind; what al-Qaeda did was to kill Americans simply for the sake of killing Americans. If that is your goal and you don't mind dying yourself to achieve it, conventional deterrence will not work. This naturally raised fears about future use of WMDs, enhanced by the actual anthrax attacks that took place in the weeks following September 11.

It was around that time that my mother, after a long decline, passed away. I drove up to State College, Pennsylvania, where she had been living in an assisted living facility for her last days, tearing myself away from what seemed like urgent discussions in Washington about the new state of the world. I had long felt guilty about not spending enough time with my mother given the pressures of work and a young family, and still have dreams where she is alive and I am neglecting to call her.

In the year and a half following the September 11 attacks, the Bush administration turned from Afghanistan to Iraq. The National Security Strategy document prepared in this period argued that it was impossible to defend against attacks whose only purpose was to kill Americans, and that the United States would henceforth need to preemptively remove threats from enemies that could make use of weapons of mass destruction. In light of the debacle that the Iraq War soon became, it is easy to forget the extraordinary fears that consumed Americans in this period. Iraq had fooled the international community already about the scope of its nuclear weapons program, anthrax had been mailed to Americans, and there were large-scale terror attacks in Spain and other countries. Iraq was already famous for its anti-imperialist radicalism and domestic cruelty, so it seemed quite plausible that it constituted a major threat to the United States.

The only problem was that Iraq was not in fact actively pursuing a WMD program at that time. No WMDs were found after the invasion; Iraq was lying in the other direction, hinting at the existence of a weapons program that it had actually dismantled. The connection between Baghdad and al-Qaeda that administration partisans were intent on seeing did not exist. While Bush linked Iraq to Iran and North Korea in an "axis of evil," the US invasion benefited Tehran enormously by destroying their Sunni Arab enemies.

Previously, I had signed one of Bill Kristol's periodic letters from the Project for the New American Century calling for US intervention to unseat Saddam Hussein. I have to admit that I did this rather casually; Bill was an old friend of mine and I hadn't been paying close attention to the situation in the Middle East in that period. While I had doubts about his anti-China positions, I had few qualms about the desirability of removing a bloodthirsty dictator from power.

I didn't break publicly with my neocon friends until February 2004, after attending a gala dinner at the American Enterprise Institute (AEI) featuring Vice President Dick Cheney, as well as my new SAIS colleague Fouad Ajami. Fouad was celebrated on the right as America's premier anti-Arab Arab; he had written a book called *The Dream Palace of the Arabs* in which he described the Arab world's self-delusions. The evening at AEI was spent celebrating what was touted as the tremendous victory that the Bush administration had achieved, at a time when Iraq was rapidly descending into a vicious civil war and American soldiers were being blown up regularly by roadside bombs. Norman Podhoretz commented at the time that there had never been so rapid an expansion of democracy in the history of US foreign policy. I came away thinking that these longtime friends of mine had taken leave of reality, leading me to write a long critique of the war for *The New York Times* that became my book *America at the Crossroads*.

In retrospect I should have written this critique much, much earlier, and should never have signed the letter advocating military action in the first place, prior to the war. I knew full well that the intervention was likely to lead to huge unintended consequences that the United States was unequipped to handle. The problem was psychological, and not a matter of policy judgment or moral disagreement. The issue was a mental block against taking a public stand against the views of longtime friends.

I changed my mind. In doing so, I began to understand why public figures change their minds so infrequently. Admitting that you were wrong would not only derail a political career and undermine your credibility; it also meant breaking with a circle of colleagues whom you regarded as part of an extended family. A couple of longtime friends, such as Vice President Cheney's chief of staff, Scooter Libby, and Eric Edelman, Undersecretary of Defense for Policy, remained in touch, but I broke off contact entirely with Bill Kristol, Paul Wolfowitz, Norman Podhoretz, and many others for what would be an extended time. I got into a public spat with the conservative columnist Charles Krauthammer, who managed to accuse me of antisemitism for my criticisms of the war. I remember a painful elevator ride with him and his wife up to a party around this time, where neither of us acknowledged the other's presence.

I don't say any of this as a matter of self-pity; breaking with friends is nothing like having your brains drilled out by an opposing militiaman, or losing your legs to an IED. The vocal advocates of the war never had to pay more than a reputational price for their actions. But this experience made me realize how important social psychology was in explaining political behavior, and how no amount of factual information could change people's opinions. Nor did native intelligence help: Paul Wolfowitz was one of the smartest people I had ever met. When I first worked for him I assumed that if he said something I didn't understand or disagreed with, it was I who was in the wrong. And yet, it sometimes takes an extremely intelligent person to convince themselves of something implausible.

So we return to the point I made at the beginning of this

story: age and social status sometimes help you change your mind, even if they make most people's views more rigid. I was at a point in life when I really didn't have to care what my old friends thought of me; I had other friends with different views and in any event was quite secure in my own skin.

Making a break over the Iraq War was actually liberating, and allowed me to shift positions on a number of completely unrelated issues. Those who supported the war tended to also believe in certain neoliberal ideas: that free markets inevitably produced good outcomes, and that governments always got in the way of growth and opportunity. These conservative ideas led to the two big disasters of the 2000s, the Iraq War and the subprime financial crisis that would unfold a few years later. The latter was the direct consequence of the deregulation of the financial sector that had occurred in stages from the late 1980s onward, culminating in the Gramm-Leach-Bliley Act of 1999 that repealed the Depression-era Glass-Steagall Act and allowed big banks to start taking huge risks. The twin failures of the war and of the financial system did a lot to discredit conservative ideas about the uses of military power and of free markets, mistakes for which America paid a huge price in the 2010s up through the present moment.

So changing my mind on the Iraq War led to a rethinking of many other areas of policy—the proper role of the state, regulation, social policy, and the like. The American efforts at nation-building in Afghanistan and Iraq led me to a long line of research over the next two decades that eventually led to my two-volume series on political order, and my firm belief in the critical importance of having a modern state.

With the rise of Donald Trump, I have finally reconciled with some old neoconservative friends, including Bill Kristol and Max Boot, both of whom became passionate Never Trumpers. They, like me, have shifted considerably to the left on economic issues since the early 2000s. Max, who had edited my op-eds for *The Wall Street Journal*, told me at one point that he was actually relieved in not having to defend conservative positions he really didn't believe in, and that I had been fortunate in breaking with them a number of years before him. At the same time, a number of people in the old neocon fraternity, such as Norman Podhoretz, turned into Trump supporters. The Straussian world, as noted earlier, had split many years earlier into East Coast and West Coast factions. Many of Harry Jaffa's West Coast followers like Michael Anton turned into Trump supporters, whose Make America Great Again had an inevitable resonance for intellectuals who were more driven by American nationalism than by philosophical ideas.

The fact that my early circle of friends—people with similar backgrounds, educations, life experiences, and, theoretically, philosophical commitments—split in such different ways has made me pessimistic about the Hegelian assertion of the growing rationality of *Geist*, or spirit. What you think and believe is so much more the contingent product of your individual psychology—your social circle, your friends, and the environment you happen to be embedded in—than a rational thought process digesting empirical information. Social rationality may appear in the long run, but we can go through prolonged periods when it is entirely missing. Perhaps this should have been obvious to me from the start, but it was a lesson painfully learned in the course of the early 2000s.

22

TALKING TO TYRANTS

MANY PEOPLE USE MEMOIRS AS AN OCCASION TO DROP names. I've met my share of world leaders, but I will spare you such a list. In general, I would note that the smaller and less influential the country, the more likely it is that I had an audience with the president or prime minister. Among them are a number of leaders who distinguished themselves as autocrats or tyrants, or were mired up to their necks in corruption. The most interesting such individual was the Libyan strongman Muammar Qaddafi.

I visited Libya twice as Qaddafi's guest in 2006 and 2007. These trips were arranged under false pretenses by the Monitor Group in Cambridge. They contacted me through, of all people, Richard Perle of Iraq War fame, who said he had just been to Tripoli and was told that Qaddafi wanted to meet with me. Libya had just dropped its WMD programs and as a consequence was taken off the US terrorism list, and there was hope that the country would end its support for revolution in Africa and the Middle East and align itself with the West. Monitor told me that they were in the business of advising Libya's leadership on market-oriented reform, but it was later revealed that they had actually signed a public relations contract to lobby on Libya's behalf. Suspecting from the beginning that this was their real motive, I never wrote anything about my visits, but this wasn't true of all of the American academics Monitor brought over.

On arriving in Tripoli, I was met by Abdullah Senussi, a brother-in-law of Muammar's who was the head of one of the country's two intelligence services. As such, he was on the international most wanted list as the mastermind of the 1988 Pan Am 103 bombing. Senussi was a heavyset, thick-necked man who looked the part of an intelligence goon; the Monitor people called him "Mr. Armani" as an ironic comment on the shiny suits he wore. He was, however, extremely tough-minded and intelligent in speaking about geopolitics in the Middle East. According to Senussi, the Wahhabis in Saudi Arabia who carried out the September 11 attacks were the greatest threat to regional peace, a greater threat than Shiite Iran. He said that a number of Libyans had gone on Hajj in Mecca and were radicalized there, and on their return had turned to violence against other Libyans. He said that even after September 11, the United States wasn't sufficiently alarmed about the long-term threat that the Saudi Wahhabis posed. That was why they were inviting a string of American opinion leaders to Tripoli, beginning with neoconservatives such as Richard Perle and the Princeton professor Bernard Lewis, who had been a big proponent of the Iraq invasion.

After an elaborate Arab lunch at Senussi's mother's house, Mr. Armani drove me in a new Toyota Land Cruiser to Sebha in the middle of the desert to meet Qaddafi in his famous tent. The tent was actually quite spacious and air-conditioned, with several large flat-panel TVs carrying CNN and some Arab news channels. I was a bit out of sorts because British Airways had managed to lose my luggage on the way to Tripoli and I'd had to buy new clothes for myself. Qaddafi in his Bedouin gear greeted me in passable English. He said that he would much rather meet with an intellectual like me than with Egypt's Hosni Mubarak or any other political leader: "You wrote an important book, and I have written an important book," meaning his *Green Book* that was required reading of everyone in Libya. He wanted to exchange notes.

Thus began several hours of one-on-one discussions (if that's what you can call them) with the Libyan dictator that extended into a second visit in early 2007. Qaddafi was a reasonably bright but extremely poorly educated military officer who had staged a coup and become dictator of his country at the age of twenty-seven. He never had any form of higher education and his head was filled with endless conspiracy theories and crazy ideas. His *Green Book* propounded a theory of direct democracy in which "basic people's congresses" would meet at a grassroots level and debate all policy issues with no higher-level representation. In fact, he attacked political representation as undemocratic. Qaddafi claimed that this would be a "third way" between US and Communist approaches, but of course it was nothing but a cover for his personal control of the country. Since he'd become a dictator at such a young age, there was never anyone to tell him that his ideas were nonsense and that he should go back to school and learn the basics.

His limitations were evident from the beginning. He had a zero-sum view of wealth: wealth could not be created, only taken from someone else. I asked him then where Bill Gates—at that time one of the richest men in the world—

got his money. Qaddafi said he stole it from his customers. I pointed out that they got useful software in return; he thought about it a bit and said that Gates stole it from the companies that made computers. But I said that these companies were themselves very wealthy, making money selling computers with Gates's software. The "Leader" then conceded that perhaps this wealth was created rather than stolen, but he quickly asserted that this could only happen in the West. In the Middle East, value only moved from one pocket to another and was never created. This actually made a certain amount of sense for a country whose only valuable product was oil that just gushed out of the ground; either you owned it or someone else did. He mentioned in a speech a couple of weeks later that in the West value could be created, and the Monitor people thought that was a big breakthrough.

On this trip I also met Saif al-Islam, Qaddafi's son, who was close to Abdullah Senussi. Saif was said to be the Qaddafi family member who was leading the reform movement and would seek to transition Libya to democracy. He lived in a house near the Tripoli airport decorated in a gaudy young Arab hipster style reminiscent of Saddam Hussein's sons' palaces. Saif was a regular customer for the direct British Airways flight from London to Tripoli, but he was perpetually late to board and the British Airways ground staff would have to hold the departure for him. They eventually got fed up with his behavior and deliberately slammed the door in his face on a subsequent flight.

Saif was at the time supposedly studying for a PhD at the London School of Economics (LSE). His foundation gave LSE a large donation and the school eventually awarded him the degree. I was told during my visit that Monitor was quietly helping him write his dissertation, and I politely declined the offer to serve as a reader. This would eventually erupt into a huge scandal when Saif gave a bloodthirsty speech during the Arab Spring, promising "rivers of blood" for the protestors demonstrating against his father. His thesis advisor, David Held, and Howard Davies, the then-director of LSE, both ended up resigning their posts, and the North African studies program they helped create with Libyan money was closed down.

I decided to quit after my second conversation with Qaddafi. While he seemed open to argument in our conversation about economics, he was totally intransigent when anyone suggested that his political system wasn't in fact the epitome of democracy. I met a number of Libyan professors and advisors who were trying to draft a new constitution. They seemed reasonably sensible and decently educated, but it was clear that the Leader himself had neither a concept of reform nor the slightest intention of moving in that direction.

LSE was rightly criticized for granting Saif a doctorate, not just because he gave a bloodthirsty speech, but due to the questionable quality of his dissertation. Many Western universities and research institutions have been going after Arab oil money for decades now in an unseemly way that can, as in Saif's case, lead to actual corruption. However, I don't think it was wrong for them to try to engage with ostensibly reform-minded Libyans in the period immediately after the lifting of sanctions. In 2006–2007 no one knew how an Arab dictatorship seeking to reform itself might have evolved. Stranger things had just happened, such as the collapse of Communism in Eastern Europe and South Africa's miraculous transition from apartheid to democracy the previous decade.

Qaddafi was poised to carry out the bloody crackdown promised by Saif in 2011 when the United States, Britain, and France intervened to stop him. This quickly led to his overthrow and murder in 2011 at the hands of a mob, which then degenerated into a bloody civil war that has continued up to the present day. Would Libya have been better off had the Western powers allowed Qaddafi to consolidate his rule, even if that meant bloodshed and repression? Some Libyans have come to feel nostalgic for Muammar's strongman rule, and Saif, after having spent time in prison, was able to run for president of the country.

Nothing better illustrates the limits of American and Western power in the Middle East than their engagement with Libya. The latter was never a nation; it was created by the Italians out of a forced unification of three Ottoman vilayets, or provinces, that wanted little to do with one another. This internal division has invited meddling by outside powers—not just the United States and the West but Russia, Turkey, the Gulf states, China, and various al-Qaeda-linked extremist groups. It may be the case that only a dictator could hold such an entity together, as the human cost of Libya's civil war has been enormous.

In the Strauss-Kojève debate mentioned earlier, Kojève asserted the Hegelian view that philosophy and politics were ultimately compatible, and that indeed philosophical wisdom had been achieved with the advent of the "universal homogenous state" that emerged at the end of history. While politics and tyranny may continue to exist in the present-day world, Kojève implied that tyrants might be brought around to accepting the principles of universal recognition enunciated during the French Revolution. Leo Strauss by contrast disagreed with Kojève and argued that there was a permanent tension between philosophy and tyranny. Politics could never be made compatible with philosophy; speaking "truth to power" as many liberals hope to do is a vain exercise.

23

THE SURGEON

QADDAFI'S LIBYA IN THE END WAS A RATHER LOW-quality dictatorship. It remains today a country without institutions that has become a failed state. China, however, has highly developed authoritarian institutions that have been around for several millennia, much longer than their Western counterparts.

I had another close encounter with an authoritarian leader when I met in 2015 with Wang Qishan, who came far closer to being a philosophically minded tyrant than Qaddafi. At that time Wang was the second-most-powerful man after Xi Jinping in the Standing Committee of the Chinese Communist Party. Xi had been in power only two years at this point. As head of the Central Commission for Discipline Inspection, Wang Qishan was leading Xi's anticorruption campaign and was the most feared man in China. He was responsible for purging the party of tens of thousands of officials both high and low—or as they put it at the time, both tigers and flies. Those caught up in the sweep included a former minister of the interior and a railway minister who was executed virtually on the spot.

To this day, it is a mystery to me how and why this meeting took place. Wang was friends with a number of foreigners, including former Treasury Secretary Hank Paulson, with whom he talked frequently. I was asked by my Stanford colleague Masahiko Aoki to go to China with him to attend a conference on the rule of law at Tsinghua University. Masa was a prominent economist at Stanford who specialized in the economies of both Japan and China, and had built his own research center in Beijing. Shortly before we arrived in China, Masa told me that we were to have an audience with Wang Qishan. The meeting had been arranged by Tatsuhito Tokuchi, a Japanese national who worked his entire life in China and was high up in the Chinese corporate world as a director of the financial firm CITIC. Masa, Tokuchi, and I were conveyed to Zhongnanhai, the compound in Beijing on Lake Beihai that houses the offices of the president, general secretary, and other high officials of the CCP.

Wang Qishan greeted us in a large room with perhaps a couple dozen other people seated behind our couches. After the meeting, a transcript appeared on the Chinese internet and then disappeared after a few days. It was claimed that the notes were taken by Tokuchi, but it is much more likely they were recorded by someone in the room and then later transcribed. This means that their release must have been intentional on Wang Qishan's part.

In *The Origins of Political Order* I argued that China was the first world civilization to create not just a centralized state but a modern state that aspired to treat its citizens impersonally. This began with the Qin unification of China in 221 BC. I spent a lot of time in that book discussing China's early dynastic history, because it seemed to me that people in the West did not appreciate the degree of state modernity that existed there some eighteen hundred years before modern states arose in Europe. China invented meritocracy and a merit-based bureaucracy. Most American experts on China focus on the country's history over the past century; their knowledge of dynastic history is often limited to the final decades of the Qing Dynasty when China was being ruled by foreigners and was in the midst of severe institutional decay.

It is hard to imagine anyone more different from Qaddafi than Wang. While both were intellectually curious, Wang Qishan was genuinely well-read, well educated, and thoughtful. Most important, he didn't see himself as an important thinker and had none of the Libyan's ridiculous narcissism about his personal role in history. He had evidently read my *Origins of Political Order* and said that it showed how elements of Chinese government were based on universal principles. He explained that he spent a lot of time reading history and noted:

> In the 1980s, when I was at the Institute of Economics, I required everyone to read history. When the institute was established, there were only a dozen people. There was no ceremony. We opened a reading list and read books for a month. The first book was "Chinese Language" from the Ming Dynasty; the second book was "The Limits to Growth of the Club of Rome" in the 1970s. A Chinese student returned to China and told me about "Democracy in America" by Tocqueville. Later, I asked them to translate it into Chinese.

Wang Qishan's introduction of Tocqueville to the CCP elite evidently had a major impact on their thinking about reform. Tocqueville's *The Old Regime and the Revolution* described how French politics was liberalized by reformers in the years prior to the French Revolution, a process that triggered rapidly rising expectations that outpaced the rate of reform. The result was the collapse of the Old Regime in 1789. The Chinese Communist Party was determined not to let something similar happen there.

I had been told prior to our meeting that Wang Qishan was very interested in American politics and would ask me a lot of questions. This did not happen; he spoke for over an hour and I was barely able to get a single question in to him. His main theme was how China was a huge country with 1.4 billion people, and that to keep it together required disciplined central authority. He said that the party itself was the only force that could correct its own mistakes, and compared the anticorruption campaign he was leading to a surgeon trying to take out his own appendix. He kept repeating that the process of modernization in China would take a very long time, and that Westerners did not appreciate the enormity of the task. The only question I succeeded in asking was whether he could ever imagine an anticorruption campaign being undertaken by an independent judiciary, which was how state wrongdoing would be policed in the United States and other Western countries. Wang replied very emphatically, "It's impossible. The judiciary must be carried out under the leadership of the party. This is the characteristic of China."

As we were leaving our audience with him, I gave him a copy of the Chinese edition of my book. He took it with a smile and said, "When I was a child, my parents told us to study hard, and now I think it makes sense. Just reading without thinking is not enough. You must study with your 'heart' . . .

A photo of a Chinese reader taken during the Covid epidemic

Confucius said, 'If you study without thinking, you will be lost; if you think without studying, you will be in danger.'"

My books, particularly the first volume of the *Political Order* series, became big bestsellers in China, and my Chinese publisher was the only one to publish my complete collected works. After I returned from China, virtually every Chinese friend I knew had read the transcript of our talk and tried to puzzle out the meaning of the encounter. The fact that many other people from the Central Commission for Discipline Inspection and the foreign experts bureau were present suggested that Wang was trying to demonstrate his loyalty to Xi and the party line. Others thought that the very fact he was meeting with me was in itself an assertion of independence and openness of mind. Some said that Xi was displeased after the fact that the meeting had taken place. Wang was removed from his position as the head of the anticorruption drive at the next party plenum, and has since faded into the background. I nonetheless get a New Year's card from him every year, specially delivered by the Chinese embassy in Washington.

24

SAMUEL P. HUNTINGTON

I NEVER ACTUALLY TOOK A COURSE WITH SAMUEL HUNtington. For most of the time in the late 1970s when I was getting my degree in the Harvard Government Department, he was in Washington working for the Carter administration. He returned to Cambridge during my final year in graduate school and gave me a scholarship at the Center for International Affairs, which he directed. I nonetheless got to know him: his many students in the field of security studies got together every summer for quite a number of years in the 1980s at the Wianno Club in Cape Cod, where he socialized and led discussions on foreign policy.

There are few political scientists who have had as profound an impact on their field as Huntington. In many of the discipline's subfields, such as comparative politics, American studies, civil-military relations, international relations, and security studies, he wrote the fundamental text that continues to be relevant to the present day.

Sam Huntington was remarkably soft-spoken and even shy for an academic of his prominence. He was not good at small talk; I remember trying to make conversation with him at receptions and not knowing quite how to fill the awkward silences that punctuated his talk. This problem resolved itself as we got to know each other better over the years; he was in the end always kind and, with one exception, supportive. He was a lifelong Democrat who served in Democratic administrations, but was temperamentally conservative, which put him at odds with much of his party by the end of his career.

Huntington's first major book was his 1968 work, *Political Order in Changing Societies*. American social science up to that point had been dominated by what was known as modernization theory, the view that development was a coherent process in which economic growth, social transformation, modern states, and egalitarian democracy were all mutually supportive and progressed in tandem. In other words, all good things went together. It was an American version of Whig history, in which postwar America was seen in many ways to be the final end point of the modernization process.

Political Order in Changing Societies undermined modernization theory, which has never thereafter recovered. Huntington pointed out that all good things do not necessarily go together. In particular, if the rate of social mobilization outpaced the ability of political institutions to accommodate new social groups, there would be political decay and the breakdown of basic order. He wrote this book against the backdrop of the coups, revolutions, and social upheavals in the developing world of the 1960s, which dashed earlier hopes that the newly independent former colonies would modernize quickly and converge with the rich world. Huntington's book was shocking to American readers because of the priority he gave to order and stability over liberal democracy: on its opening page, he asserted that both the United States and the Soviet Union were equally developed societies because of their ability to provide order.

When I wrote *The End of History and the Last Man* in 1992, I had not yet read Huntington. I began my two-volume series, *The Origins of Political Order* and *Political Order and Political Decay*, in an effort to update not just his book but my own as well. I took as my starting point Huntington's insight that economic growth and political development were two separate processes that did not necessarily support each other. I also accepted his view that having a coherent modern state was important regardless of whether that state was liberal and democratic, and that political order had precedence over democracy. My own work up to that point had not sufficiently separated democracy and rule-of-law institutions from the state, and underemphasized the importance of the latter. In the decade following the end of the Cold War, there were plenty of transitions to democracy in the sense of countries holding elections, but many fewer transitions to modern states that were impersonal and had the capacity to be effective. The failure to modernize the state then undermined the stability and quality of democracy, as new democracies around the world failed to promote growth and opportunity, or else were mired in corruption.

In 1993, Sam Huntington published "The Clash of Civilizations" in *Foreign Affairs*; this became the 1996 book *The Clash of Civilizations and the Remaking of World Order*. For the next couple of decades, students in introductory classes in international relations all over the world were made to read his article alongside "The End of History?"

After the events of the early 2000s, many people would say that his perspective of clashing cultures in which liberal democracy was simply one of several choices was the superior one. The liberal world order that had been dominant after the fall of Communism has been in retreat since about 2008, and there has been democratic backsliding everywhere, including in the United States. But this didn't necessarily mean that Sam was right about the world that would eventually emerge. *The Clash of Civilizations* was very much rooted in the rise of Islamism after the 1979 Iranian Revolution, when it looked like the world was headed toward a broad conflict between Muslim countries and those aligned with the West. This view seemed to receive affirmation with the al-Qaeda attacks on September 11 and the spread of militant Islam. His fundamental view, one that he elaborated in subsequent books, was that culture, as defined by the world's major religious traditions, would be the organizing principle of global politics.

But this is not the defining characteristic of the world we live in today. In the various critiques I wrote concerning Huntington's thesis, I noted that it was only in the Muslim world that anyone thinks in civilizational terms. The challenge posed by militant Islam that seemed so threatening in the 2000s still exists in poor regions such as the Sahel, but has receded significantly everywhere else. Radical Islam was heavily promoted by Saudi Arabia after the regime was shaken by the attack on the Grand Mosque in late 1979, but under the country's current ruler, Mohammed bin Salman, Saudi policy has shifted in a more liberal direction. The Muslim world is not a cohesive bloc; the primary rift runs within it as Sunnis and Shias have contested for power.

People in the West moreover don't identify primarily as citizens of "Christendom." Nor do the Chinese, Japanese, and Koreans believe they are part of a single Confucian civilization as they fight over historical legacies. Russia and Ukraine share a common Orthodox culture, which hasn't prevented them from fighting a bitter war since 2014. There is today a growing alliance between Russia, China, Iran, and North Korea, with Venezuela and Nicaragua attaching themselves as minor players. They all represent different civilizations, in Huntington's terms; what keeps them together is their common opposition to a liberal democratic world led by the United States. While liberal democracy may have been on its back foot for the last couple of decades, it still remains the chief ideology being contested around the world. Rather than culture, it is ideology, combined with a bit of realpolitik calculation, that shapes contemporary geopolitics.

When the book version of *The Clash of Civilizations* first came out, I wrote a critical review of it in *The Wall Street Journal*. Sam was upset by this and didn't speak to me for about a year. We eventually reconciled, however, particularly after I began my project to resurrect interest in his *Political Order in Changing Societies*. Sam's lifelong interest in culture as a factor in politics did not end; his last book, *Who Are We?*, on American national identity, pointed to the importance of Protestantism in shaping both American democracy and culture. His critique of immigration from Latin America led progressives to denounce him as an academic precursor to Donald Trump.

This was unfair. There is no question that modern democracy is supported by certain cultural values. As Marty Lipset explained, sectarian Protestantism played a huge role in shaping modern Western attitudes toward individualism, equality, human rights, and democracy itself. The abolitionist movement was led before the Civil War by Protestant ministers, as was the Civil Rights Movement in the 1960s. African American ministers such as Martin Luther King Jr. drew inspiration from the Christian tradition they grew up in. Not all cultures are equally friendly to liberal and democratic practices.

Sam Huntington was simply pointing out that there were cultures that were not as supportive of liberal values as America's Protestant one. Where he was mistaken, in my opinion, was not in this abstract view of the importance of culture, but rather in underestimating the degree to which cultures are capable of change. The Hispanic immigrants coming into the United States in recent decades are no further separated from mainstream Anglo culture than were the immigrants from Southern Italy at the turn of the twentieth century, who after a generation or so were successfully assimilated into the American mainstream. Sam had argued that the Protestant work ethic was key to America's success. As I said in one of my critiques, no one in America works harder than recent immigrants from Guatemala or Korea or Iran, and certainly not the privileged descendants of the Anglo elite with their legacy gateways into elite universities. Culture matters, but it is also malleable.

25

BUILDING THINGS II

FURNITURE WAS NOT THE ONLY THING I LIKED TO build. Beginning in the mid-1990s, I started assembling my own PCs. Windows-based computers are not hard to build. You just buy the parts—motherboard, CPU, memory, disk storage, case, monitor, and graphics card, and plug them together. There are a number of little tricks you learn along the way, such as properly seating the cooling fan on top of the microprocessor, or inserting the memory sticks into their sockets the right way. But PCs are highly modular and standardized, and the standards don't shift that often—from SCSI connectors to SATA to NVMe, or from DDR3 to DDR4, or DVI to DisplayPort to connect the monitor. You just need to keep straight what the current standards are, and buy accordingly.

This hobby merged seamlessly with my woodworking. When I got my first teaching job at George Mason University in 1995, I had access to educational versions of a lot of high-powered software such as Autodesk's AutoCAD, which I then used to design the furniture I wanted to build out of wood. Those 2D blueprints soon turned into 3D virtual objects that could be rotated and realistically rendered; I built a virtual Georgian house in which I could place my Federal furniture.

I didn't just build hardware. I have programmed computers for much of my adult life, starting with a version of Microsoft Basic that ran on my first Kaypro II computer. I moved from Basic to Pascal and then to C and Java. I wrote an armored maneuver warfare simulator in Pascal that replicated logistics trains and allowed smart commanders to win battles by cutting supply lines. In the 1990s, complex adaptive systems were becoming trendy, so I wrote an agent-based model in Java (called Agent, strangely enough) that simulated creatures swimming around in a tank. The creatures could eat, find each other, mate, have babies, and eventually die of starvation or old age. These days, I do all my coding in Python, which is a wonderfully flexible programming language. I use my own software regularly to maintain databases, build outlines, and interact with other programs. It turns out that Claude Code is a great tool for programmers; you tell it what you want the program to do in natural language, and the AI spits out the code. Like many high school kids, I've built robots, drones, and remote-controlled vehicles using Arduinos and Raspberry Pis, and build 3D models with Fusion 360. My latest project has been a Proxmox server that hosts a dozen virtual machines, including a Linux distribution called Kali that is optimized for hackers.

I know of few things as satisfying as hitting the "on" switch of a complex system you've been building for a couple of weeks and its doing what it's supposed to, or pressing the "compile" button on your computer and getting a functioning software program. There's no ambiguity as to your success, as there is in writing an essay or giving a lecture.

But there is a deeper reason for getting into technology at

a level beyond what's in a given product's operating manual. It has to do with personal autonomy. In modern society we are all extremely dependent on technological systems, for the most part designed by huge, distant technology companies. We are dependent on those companies, and therefore subject to manipulation by them in ways that we scarcely understand. When we do a search on the internet, or see a news feed, or order something online, our experience is shaped by complex algorithms designed to foster the company's self-interest. We may benefit as a result, but no one should be under any illusion that the company has our interest primarily in mind.

This is why I've always disliked Apple products, even though I've owned them in the past and have an iPhone and iPad. From the standpoint of someone who wants to maximize his technological autonomy, Apple computers are an absolute nightmare. Apple products were deliberately designed to prevent their users from modifying them, down to the use of proprietary fasteners that require special Apple-only tools to open the case. Apple does not want you to be able to fix or modify your own computer—rather, it wants you to visit the Genius Bar at the Apple Store and look over all the new products while you wait for someone to fix your machine in the back room. The "genius" refers not to you, the helpless customer, but to the marketing guy who thought up this system.

You can never totally escape dependence and manipulation by these big companies. But the more you know about the underlying technology, the more you can understand the ways you are being manipulated, and take some steps to protect yourself. Things go wrong with computers all the time, and it's good to be able to know how to get them working again yourself. And in the future, it may be a matter of survival. Our current technological world is actually quite fragile, dependent on the interoperation of a host of extremely complex systems. It is very easy to imagine future states of the world in which one or more of these systems stops working, leading to a cascade of other failures. Think what would happen if the Global Positioning System (GPS) went down, or perhaps the international GNSS system, through a rogue electromagnetic pulse (EMP) blast. No one knows how to read maps anymore, and paper maps are hard to find. One of the worrying things about the current rush to build ever-bigger AI systems is that we will be delegating the oversight of these systems to a yet more complex machine, whose designers themselves don't have a clear idea of why it is working the way it is. At that point, our ability to respond to a failure may be out of our hands, and we will have to revert to an earlier level of technology. People used to be able to repair their own gasoline-powered cars, but the likelihood that they could repair a self-driving car or robotaxi is virtually nil. Their owners will be completely dependent on some large, unapproachable tech company, which may itself have gone out of business, to keep them working. Knowledge about those earlier technologies may come in handy at that point.

26

CANCIÓN PARA MI AMÉRICA

I WROTE MY DOCTORAL DISSERTATION ON SOVIET foreign policy in the Middle East, and spent most of the first decade of my career doing research on and traveling to the former Soviet Union. However, the part of the world I have visited the most often since then, and the one I enjoy the most, is Latin America.

Coming out of graduate school, I knew little about this region. Americans tend to pay attention to Latin America only when it causes problems, such as civil wars in the 1980s and drugs and immigration up to the present. The academics who specialize in Latin American politics tended to be on the left, and saw the countries there as victims of American imperialism. Beginning in the late 1980s, however, a number of libertarians on the right also took an interest in the region. Chile after the overthrow of Pinochet had become a laboratory for their free-market ideas. Anyone interested in the fate of democracy globally needs to pay attention to the Western Hemisphere, because this is where most of the world's democracies are located.

My first visits were to Brazil and Argentina in the early 1990s. Both countries at that time were coming out of dictatorship and debt. When I visited Brazil in 1991, the country had chosen its first civilian president just six years previously, ending the military dictatorship that seized power in a 1964 coup. Brazil was still suffering from inflation, running at around 20 percent per month under President Fernando Collor. I thought this was an impossibly high rate, but when I got to Buenos Aires a few months later I was told by my Argentine hosts that Brazil had never experienced a true hyperinflation. Argentina's inflation rate in 1989–90 at one point reached over 4,000 percent per year. Under those circumstances, they explained, if you were paid on a Friday, you immediately went to the store and bought as many groceries as possible, since prices would be significantly higher on Monday.

Argentina struck me back then as a country trying to pretend it was located somewhere in southern Europe and accidentally got towed to a different part of the world. Just as in Western Europe fifty years ago, there was little apparent racial diversity and the country prided itself on its concert pianists, tango, and tennis players. President Carlos Menem was elected in 1989 and positioned himself as a daring neoliberal reformer who would tame the country's inflation and reengage with the democratic world after the disastrous Falklands War with Britain. I was taken to dinner my first night there by a group of Menem's followers who had come with him from La Rioja Province, where he had been governor. They themselves seemed disoriented by both the change of venue to the capital, and the change in economic ideology that their boss had embraced.

Brazil, by contrast, was far more multiracial, and the staples of Brazilian culture such as samba and the Carnival manifest many more African influences. I had also just recently visited South Africa for the first time as that country was turning to democracy, and found Brazil much more likable. There is of course a lot of racism in Brazil—the professional elites you meet are almost all white and European. But the white South Africans under apartheid had created a fantasy world in which they could pretend that the Black population didn't exist, tucked away as it was in invisible townships. Brazil was very different. The elegant silver-haired Englishman who escorted me around explained that he decided to stay in Rio after a visit because Brazilian women were so beautiful and sex was so available. He waxed lyrical about a mulatta he was dating, the sort of thing I never heard in Johannesburg.

Carlos Menem turned out to be a huge disappointment. Neoliberalism has fallen out of favor in Latin America, and has become a punching bag for many on the left. But there are times and places where neoliberal remedies are actually right and necessary, and Argentina in the 1990s was one of them. Menem and his economy minister, Domingo Cavallo, actually succeeded in getting the country's inflation rate back down from the disastrous hyperinflation of the late 1980s, but Menem never followed through on important reforms such as reducing the size of Argentina's bloated public sector. When Cavallo returned to the economics ministry in the late 1990s, he made a number of mistakes that set the scene for the country's collapse in 2001. It has been left to a more radical libertarian, Javier Milei, elected in 2023, to complete the agenda Menem started.

My naïveté about Latin America was on full display during an early visit to Bogotá, sometime in the mid- to late 1990s. After I arrived the defense minister explained to me how the country had been deeply embroiled in a war against the FARC and Pablo Escobar's Medellín cartel, something I was at the time only dimly aware of. I was to give a speech to ANDI, the Colombian employers' federation, about the geopolitics of the region. The talk was carried live on national television, and in the front row was the then-president, Ernesto Samper. I casually mentioned that Colombia had become famous as the locus of the hemispheric drug trade, not knowing that Samper was accused of taking money from the drug cartels to fund his presidential campaign. I wanted to hide under a rock after my talk when I was told that my words had been broadcast all across Colombia, and that I had in effect insulted the president of the country to his face on national TV. I assumed my hosts at ANDI would be furious and embarrassed.

As it turned out later that evening, my sponsors were delighted. The business elite was disgusted with Samper and believed that he was a disgrace to Colombia. They explained to me how deeply corrupt the president was, and that he had to be stopped from infecting the entire state administration. They were quite happy to see him humiliated by a gringo.

This was the first of many trips I've taken to Colombia. The country is fascinating: it has a highly educated middle class, good universities, and a cosmopolitan professional elite. Yet if you venture just a few kilometers outside of Bogotá or Medellín, you are cast back many decades into a highly impoverished rural society beset by drugs, narco-traffickers, paramilitaries, and high levels of violence. There was a prolonged period of civil war in the late 1940s and early 1950s, known as *la violencia*, which led many rural Colombians to flee to large barrios in cities such as Medellín and Cali. Escobar created a virtual state-within-a-state in Medellín as he profited off the US cocaine market in the 1980s. Colombia was not able to control the escalating violence even after Escobar was killed in 1993. That year Medellín's murder rate reached some 400 per 100,000 population, higher than Mexico in the 2000s or any US inner city at any time.

During the early 2000s, it looked like important parts of Latin America were on the verge of transformation: Mexico and Brazil were led by center-right politicians, the Central American civil wars had mostly finished, and there was some progress being made in reducing the region's levels of inequality. I was invited to Brazil by a Nelson Fukuyama, whose grandfather, like mine, had emigrated from Fukuoka Prefecture in the early years of the twentieth century—but to São Paulo rather than LA. We watched as one Chinese bulk carrier after another loaded up at the port of Santos. But then, everything came crashing down in the 2010s. The global financial crisis cut into commodity exports; Brazil, Argentina, and Mexico grew more polarized and spawned populist politicians; and Venezuela turned into an utter disaster, with a GDP drop of two-thirds and 8 million people leaving the country in the following decade.

The fundamental problem in Latin America was and continues to be the region's economic and social inequality—the highest level of any region in the world. The reasons for this are deeply buried in the Spanish and Portuguese colonial legacy: Europeans came to the region hoping to extract gold, silver, and other precious metals, and later turned to plantation crops such as sugar. The slave trade was born in the seventeenth and eighteenth centuries in the triangular trade between Africa, northeastern Brazil, the Caribbean, and the American South. The northern half of the United States practiced a much more egalitarian form of family farming, by contrast, and defeated the southern half in the Civil War. Latin America might be thought of as what the United States would be had the South never been defeated. Slavery would likely have died out throughout the hemisphere over time, but the social hierarchies it bequeathed would have survived in a much starker form. The radicalism of the Republican Party at the time of the Civil War pushed US society in a more egalitarian direction. As an example, the Argentine military dictator Juan Manuel de Rosas rose to power in Buenos Aires Province in the 1860s. He became a landowner and encouraged the formation of large haciendas for his friends and family. That landed elite participated in the overthrow of Argentina's democracy in 1930, and has been a base of support for authoritarian leaders since then. Rosas lived in the same period that Abraham Lincoln and the Republican Party in the United States passed the Homestead Act that opened up the American West to family farming. The Republicans also passed the Morrill Act, which created a network of land-grant universities all over the country, raising productivity and education levels. America has not been plagued by a reactionary landed elite to nearly the same extent as Argentina and other Latin American countries.

Liberal democracy and open economies have consequently had a much more checkered history in Latin America in the years since then. Democracies were overthrown all across the region in the 1960s and 1970s, with regime opponents disappearing or being thrown out of helicopters. The authoritarian temptation remains powerful despite the restoration of democracy that occurred in the 1970s and 1980s, and is full-blown in Venezuela, Nicaragua, and Cuba.

State weakness continues to be a huge problem. The Mexican government today does not have a monopoly of legitimate force; a number of states are effectively controlled by narcomafias and politicians deeply embroiled in corruption. The impact that state-building can have is nowhere more evident than in Colombia, which, as noted earlier, never had a state that could exercise a monopoly of violence throughout its whole territory. The national state began to reclaim control from the FARC and other armed groups only in the early 2000s.

But the transformation of the city of Medellín was not simply due to the use of military force. It was based on an entirely new approach to the relationship between government and citizen brought on by a new generation of politicians. Once the constitution was amended in 1993, mayors were elected rather than appointed by the national government. This degree of local control facilitated the rise of politicians such as Sergio Fajardo, a mathematics professor trained at the University of Wisconsin who as mayor of the city promised reform of social policy. He installed a cable car system that went up the sides of the barrios where the poor lived, connecting them to the city's new metro system and allowing them to fly over the gangs that previously prevented them from getting to work in the middle-class parts of the city. He hired famous European architects to build structures such as the Biblioteca España in some of the poorest neighborhoods of the city, demonstrating to inhabitants that they were visible to the municipal government. This increased level of trust allowed for better policing, and together with the more forceful policies undertaken against the drug gangs by the police and army, the levels of violence began to drop markedly.

This transformation was not solely dependent on government, national or municipal. Civil society was very active in the poor neighborhoods, providing social services; the business community helped out by being willing to pay higher taxes, and the universities provided policy advice and analysis. Things in the city were well run; the public utility, Empresas Públicas de Medellín, actually made money that could be used to fund social programs, unlike the vast majority of developing-country public utilities. None of this made much of a dent in the drug trade, which was driven by the huge demand coming from North America, but these efforts did cut the level of violence significantly.

Riding the cable car up to Comuna Uno, the barrio hosting the Biblioteca España, I felt some degree of shame and embarrassment. There are many American cities beset by drugs and gangs where public policy has been able to make little headway in improving the lives of citizens. In Medellín there was a shared commitment to civic life, as well as a local government that was both accountable and accessible. Something like this could have been done in, say, Baltimore, the setting for the HBO series *The Wire*. But many of the pieces were missing: a competent and uncorrupt municipality, a middle class that actually wanted to solve the problem rather than fleeing to the suburbs, and above all a high degree of imagination when it came to new ways of dealing with social problems.

These are hopeful trends, and there are others. The region is much more accepting of diversity than other parts of the world. Peru had a Japanese president, Argentina and El Salvador have had Arab leaders, and Mexico now has a Jewish woman chief executive. Despite bad actors such as Venezuela and Nicaragua, it has remained democratic through financial crises and Covid. Outside of Europe and North America, it remains the most democratic region. Latin America has seen the rise of populists of both the Left and the Right, but it has also seen genuine successes like that of Medellín as well.

27

ON SOCIAL THEORY

FOR MUCH OF MY ACADEMIC LIFE I'VE HAD A LOVE-HATE relationship with the discipline of economics. It is impossible to exist in the modern world without economics and economists: they gather data, have sophisticated tools for analyzing it, and provide the empirical foundation for any kind of public policy. Many nonacademics complain about ivory-tower theorizing, but it is impossible to live in the world without theory. Every politician in Congress wants a policy to do something: improve airline safety, reduce gang violence, assure drug safety, enhance educational outcomes. Even as they decry academic theory, they themselves act on the basis of an often unarticulated theory that says, "If we do X, then Y will follow."

The problem is not with theorizing, but with the fact that most theories are pulled out of people's back pockets, usually driven by an anecdote or personal experience. Indeed, with the rise of the internet, theories are literally pulled out of the ether; if the theory gets enough "likes" or is endorsed by a popular influencer, it is considered confirmed.

Economists are a critical antidote to this sort of unsystematic theorizing. Their raison d'être is to be rigorously empirical, and to develop a battery of tools that allow them to make causal inferences based on good empirical data. This doesn't mean that they don't betray hidden biases or get things wrong, sometimes big-time. But it is infinitely preferable to rely on this kind of empirical social science than on random opinions heard on the internet.

The problem I have with economists lies in a different direction, and is twofold. The first is that in their search for methodological rigor, they fail to address some of the most important questions, and fail to appreciate the importance of other approaches to knowledge. And the second is that their underlying model of human behavior is woefully limited.

The former problem became clear to me from personal experience. In the late 1990s, there was a lot of interest among social scientists in the questions of social trust and social capital, and economists weighed in with both data gathering and empirical analysis. After the publication of *Trust*, I was invited to a number of conferences on the subject. One was attended by the Nobel laureate economist Robert Solow, whose "Solow growth theory" was one of the foundational models in development economics. He was clearly irked by the fact that I was at the table, and at one point he made a dismissive comment about "casual empiricism" in response to something I said. I responded that some of the great social theorists of the nineteenth century were also "casual empiricists." He scoffed at this and asked who they were. I replied, "Alexis de Tocqueville and Max Weber."

The search for methodological rigor in making causal inferences has greatly reduced the scope of the kinds of questions that can be addressed by economics. For much of the 2010s and 2020s, the favored methodology in the field has been to do randomized experiments of the sort that have long been applied in pharmaceutical trials. The social scientist will roll out an intervention to a treatment population, and compare the results to a matched control group that does not receive the intervention. This is the gold standard for achieving the highest level of certainty with regard to "X causes Y"-type assertions. But this method is of little use in answering big questions such as "What makes some countries rich and others poor?" or "Why are levels of trust so much lower in Southern than in Northern Italy?"

One of my greatest intellectual pleasures was the discovery of eighteenth- and nineteenth-century social theory. Neither neoclassical economists nor Straussians are typically fans of this genre of writing. I started reading into this literature with *Trust*, but turned to it much more systematically when I wrote *The Origins of Political Order*. This group includes Adam Smith, David Hume, Karl Marx, Émile Durkheim, Henry Maine, Numa Denis Fustel de Coulanges, Ferdinand Tönnies, and Max Weber. There are also a number of prominent twentieth-century theorists I would add to this group, including Joseph Schumpeter, Karl Polanyi, Ernest Gellner, and Albert O. Hirschman.

All of these individuals were guilty of "casual empiricism." None of them used high-powered statistical techniques to come to their conclusions, or presented so much as a simple regression. They thought about causal relationships, such as Weber's famous hypothesis about Calvinism and the origins of modern capitalism. But not one of these individuals could "prove" their conclusions in ways that would be acceptable to a modern methodologist. The majority of them wrote before the rise of modern neoclassical economics and what we understand today as social science. They would be classified rather as social theorists, and their big contributions were conceptual rather than empirical.

These concepts have been critical to the way we think about the world today. Adam Smith laid out the role of incentives in promoting economic growth and the central importance of the division of labor; David Hume spoke of the "tragedy of the commons"; Karl Marx invented the concept of social class; Maine introduced the contrast between status and contract; Durkheim was the first to speak of anomie as a condition of modern life; we owe our understanding of bureaucracy and charismatic authority to Max Weber. Smith, Marx, and Durkheim were in a prolonged conversation with one another across the decades over the meaning of the division of labor. In 1887 the German theorist Ferdinand Tönnies used the terms *Gemeinschaft* and *Gesellschaft* to describe the transition from a small, kin-based agrarian community to a modern, urban, industrial society. The American sociologist Robert Nisbet once remarked that his entire field was one long elaboration of the Tönnies dichotomy. The same transition that Tönnics saw happening in late nineteenth-century Germany took place in late twentieth-century China after Deng Xiaoping's market reforms.

The second major problem I've had with contemporary economists is their underlying model of human behavior. Neoclassical economics begins with the premise that human beings are "rational utility maximizers." In crude terms, this means that human beings are selfish but rational; they can cooperate with other human beings, but ultimately will do so out of self-interest. Many economists will argue that their concept of utility is elastic, and that many people include the well-being of others within their individual "utility functions." In recent years, economists have taken to studying topics such as altruism, religious belief, and other sorts of behaviors that wouldn't fit neatly under a materialist framework. Behavioral economics has challenged the model's assumption of rationality, showing that people make choices based on habit, social pressure, and other nonmaterial factors.

Nonetheless, the explanatory power of neoclassical economics depends heavily on the primacy of individual self-interest. If a person can both desire material things and also desire those same things for another individual, then the model will obviously have trouble predicting the choices that person will make. The deviations from pure rationality studied by behavioral economists tend to be rather small-bore, such as choosing the default option rather than closely studying alternatives. These insights lead to the ability to change behavior not in major ways but in little "nudges."

The problem with even the most expansive of these economic models lies in their assumptions about both utility and rationality. They do not take account of *thymos* and the desire for recognition as a third part of the soul besides reason and desire. *Thymos* may at times help individuals achieve their material ends, but often it works at cross-purposes with desire fulfillment. People will reject a welfare payment or a charitable gift if they are proud and don't want to be thought of as indigent or unable to provide for themselves. Rational utility maximization does not take into account Kojève's violent struggle to the death, or why some people are willing to risk their lives for higher causes.

The model of human rationality, even as modified by behavioral economics, does not explain the centrality of motivated reasoning. As Jonathan Haidt and other social psychologists have shown, human beings do not simply take in empirical facts, process them, and draw conclusions accordingly. Rather, they start with the conclusions they would like to believe, and use their cognitive abilities to cherry-pick facts that support them. This was the case with many of my friends at the time of the Iraq War. The inability of people to accept basic facts that contradict their favored outcomes has been one of the biggest challenges in contemporary politics.

I arrived at Stanford in 2010, prior to the advent of randomized experiments as the dominant methodological approach. The craze at the time was "rational choice" political science, in which economic models were applied directly to the study of politics. States were assumed to be predatory and interested only in maximizing the resources they extracted from the societies they governed. The central question to be addressed was how elites could "credibly commit" to institutions, such as a rule of law, that would limit their predation.

This approach struck me from the beginning as both excessively economistic and also very American. It began with the assumption that states were power maximizers and that the central problem of politics was how to limit that power. There was no thought as to how that power was developed in the first place, or whether power wasn't simply predatory but necessary to serve public interest. The game theoretic models that were employed were based entirely on the interactions of elites; nowhere in this model were there ordinary people who could be mobilized by ideas such as freedom and equality.

Today, rational choice political science has fallen out of favor. So little of American politics seems to be driven by the rationality assumed by this model; people have been voting against their material self-interest in ways that are better explained by social psychologists than by economists. In many corners of society, not just in the United States but in other countries, distrust of the state has metastasized into a series of extraordinarily implausible conspiracy theories that are nonetheless believed by large numbers of people.

Economists tend to be so rigidly empirical that they are afraid to say anything that goes even slightly beyond what's in their dataset, even if it's blindingly obvious. Straussians by contrast tend to be contemptuous of social science as a whole and of "mere empiricism," and often trip over themselves when speaking about the real world. The great age of social theory is a good antidote to both approaches.

28

MONSTERS, NOT SO COLD

THE INVASIONS OF IRAQ AND AFGHANISTAN ENGENdered a major shift in my own intellectual interests and research, which has lasted up to the present. I became interested in "the state."

The American invasions led to the collapse of the governments in both countries, leaving the United States with the responsibility for maintaining basic order and reestablishing some sort of state. The great German sociologist Max Weber defined the state as a monopoly of legitimate force over a defined territory. Neither of these conditions applied in either Afghanistan or Iraq: there was no monopoly of force, and no legitimacy accorded those in ostensible control. The United States found itself in the situation of having to create states from scratch, and it became clear—to me, at any rate—that the officials running the intervention had no idea how to do this.

This is where the deeply rooted American anti-statism that Marty Lipset had written so much about became a real liability. Americans never spent much time thinking about how to create legitimate state authority but needed to do so now. The Taliban regime in Kabul and that of Saddam Hussein had collapsed entirely. Who then could exercise legitimate authority? The Bush administration had illusions that an out-of-touch émigré named Ahmad Chalabi could lead a democracy, but failed to understand that democracy required prior institutions that could secure order, provide services, and collect taxes. Creating a modern, effective state was a much more difficult task than creating a democracy.

The United States had engaged in state-building a number of times previously with little success—in the Philippines at the turn of the twentieth century, in Nicaragua in the 1930s, in Vietnam in the 1960s, and indeed in the American South during Reconstruction. The authors of the Iraq War did not know what they did not know: they expected institutions of a modern state to spring up spontaneously, including functioning markets, a court system, police, and protections for private property. But such institutions are hard to create, especially in societies beset by burgeoning civil war.

The intellectual deficit went further than the Bush administration. My home discipline of political science at that point had not spent a lot of time thinking about how to organize state institutions and make them run effectively. There was a time earlier in the twentieth century when the field of public administration had been one of the four main branches of political science, bolstered by the prestige of one of its great practitioners, Woodrow Wilson. But the field was ejected in later years as unworthy of study by serious scholars, and it became its own subdiscipline. Public administration never thereafter garnered much interest, and elite schools such as Harvard and Stanford did not have departments dedicated to its study. The big issue that political scientists were struggling to understand was how to *limit* the power of a state, and not how to create that power in the first place.

One of the chapter titles in *The End of History and the Last Man* used a quote from Nietzsche's *Thus Spoke Zarathustra* that described the state as "the coldest of all cold monsters," which ruthlessly crushed peoples and their diverse "languages of good and evil." Many around the world indeed think of "the state" as a cold monster, an institution that inspires fear and distrust. One of the most popular authors read widely by political scientists in those years was the Yale anthropologist James C. Scott, whose books chronicled abuses of state power across time and space, and who extolled the virtues of stateless societies such as those in the highlands of Southeast Asia. In making his pitch for anarchy he effectively joined hands with American libertarians.

Afghanistan and Iraq in the early 2000s were both stateless societies, and they did not look nearly as peaceful and happy.

I am frequently asked how I would rewrite *The End of History and the Last Man* if I had it to do all over again. The fact of the matter is that I did rewrite that book; this took the form of my two-volume *Political Order* series that was published in the wake of the occupations of Afghanistan and Iraq. And one of the biggest issues that I neglected in the earlier book, an issue whose significance I understand much better now, is the importance of having a modern state. Up through the 1990s, however, I had been happy to blame social dysfunctions such as low trust on abuses of state power.

Anti-statism was baked into "neoliberal" economics. The Chicago School saw excessive state interference in the economy as the source of low growth and lack of innovation. The so-called Washington Consensus, reflecting economic conventional wisdom in those years, pushed for trade liberalization, deregulation, and privatization as keys to economic growth. Withdrawal of an excessively controlling state was indeed what stimulated growth in China and India. As governments in these countries began to recognize and protect private property rights, individuals could keep the fruits of their labor and productivity began to rise. Many countries in Latin America and sub-Saharan Africa that had succumbed to debt crisis in the 1980s took the harsh medicine of structural adjustment, stabilized their currencies and budgets, and were able to start growing once again.

Opinion began to turn away from strict neoliberal orthodoxy by the late 1990s, however. There were many sources of this. Many attempted transitions to market economics in post-Communist countries failed, because they lacked states that could impartially enforce a rule of law. Paradoxically, you need a strong state to privatize a state-owned enterprise; there have to be clear and strictly enforced transparency rules, open auctions, and safeguards against insider capture of the bidding process. None of this was in place in Russia, Ukraine, Georgia, or other parts of the former USSR, and as a result former state-owned enterprises were captured by insiders who became the oligarchs who continue to thrive thirty years later.

There was, moreover, a growing recognition that fast-growing countries in East Asia such as Japan, South Korea, and Taiwan had not gotten to where they were by playing by neoliberal rules. They protected private property rights and set up legal systems, but in each case implemented state-directed industrial policies that favored certain sectors over others. Governments in Asia directed credit to businesses and shielded them from foreign competition until they were strong enough to stand on their own. Many developing countries had tried import substitution and infant industry protection, but they did not have the high-quality state institutions of Japan, South Korea, Taiwan, or, ultimately, China, and as a result failed.

Finally, the United States was hoisted with its own petard in the global financial crisis of 2008. The United States and the Bretton Woods institutions over which it exercised heavy influence (the IMF in particular) had started to counsel poor countries to open their capital accounts and allow foreign investment money to flow in freely. At their urging, the global financial system was liberalized in the 1980s and 1990s, including banking reform in the United States itself that removed many of the Depression-era regulatory shackles such as the Glass-Steagall Act that limited bank risk-taking. Neoliberalism failed most grievously in the financial sector, as trillions of dollars of liquid capital began flowing into developing countries and into sectors such as the US subprime market, and flowed out again when investor sentiment changed. There were suddenly a cascading series of financial crises: Britain and Sweden in the early 1990s, Mexico a couple of years later, the Asian financial crisis in 1997, Russia and Argentina at the turn of the millennium, and finally the subprime crisis in the United States in 2008.

All of this led to a reevaluation of the importance of the state in a modern economy. States could be obstacles to growth, but they also performed critical functions in making and enforcing the rules under which private companies acted.

This shift was marked by the World Bank's 1997 World Development Report, titled *The State in a Changing World*, which heralded that institution's recognition that governments play a critical and often irreplaceable role in promoting economic growth. The bank's agenda, marked by President James Wolfensohn's 1996 "cancer of corruption" speech, shifted from deregulation and privatization to good governance and anticorruption. This was the intellectual backdrop against which my own recognition of the centrality of modern states occurred.

International order and security in those years rested completely on the existence of capable states that could control terrorism in their territories or provide basic services without high levels of corruption. This was the essential problem facing American foreign policy in "ungoverned spaces" such as Afghanistan and Iraq, and the post-Soviet countries moving away from Communism. This practical challenge was what led me to a stream of writing on the state, and to travel to many countries where states, much less modern ones, did not exist.

29

WONTOKS

AFGHANISTAN AND IRAQ WERE NOT THE ONLY SOCIEties suffering from lack of a modern state in the early 2000s. There was a lot of instability in Melanesia, the island region north and east of Australia. East Timor had just broken off as a sovereign country from Indonesia after a bloody war of national liberation; Papua New Guinea (PNG), the eastern half of the large island sitting north of Australia across the Torres Strait, was experiencing violence and unrest; and the Solomon Islands were occupied by an international peacekeeping force, the Regional Assistance Mission to Solomon Islands (RAMSI), after fighting broke out among youth factions. Just as in the Middle East, political stability would depend on the establishment of states that could provide a base level of security across their territory. I was asked by the World Bank and AusAID, the Australian Agency for International Development, to go to the region and look at the different governance programs that the international community had put in place. So began my first direct encounter with truly tribal societies.

The word "tribalism" is thrown around a lot to denote any

affinity group that is bound together by strong emotional ties. People in Kenya or Nigeria describe their problem as one of tribalism, but what they are describing is a more modern phenomenon of ethnicity politics. Americans who characterize the red-blue polarization as "tribalism" are describing something yet again different.

Tribalism properly understood is a phenomenon that anthropologists refer to as a system of segmentary lineages, in which groups of people trace descent to a common ancestor. The lineage can get larger or smaller depending on how many generations back that common ancestor lived; one of its great advantages is that the lineage can swell or shrink depending on requirements of the moment. Segmentary lineages are held together by ancestor worship, or the belief that dead progenitors can affect the well-being of their descendants in the present day, as well as their unborn children. The practice of visiting an ancestor's grave with a food offering, as in Mexico's Day of the Dead or the tomb-sweeping ceremonies in Taiwan, is a manifestation of this belief. The ancestors' spirits are often believed to be residing physically in the ground where they are buried, and will haunt disrespectful offspring.

True tribalism has largely disappeared in sub-Saharan Africa, but it still exists in parts of the Middle East, and is in full force in much of Melanesia. This is why anthropologists in previous decades loved traveling to the PNG highlands, since they could observe largely pristine segmentary lineages firsthand.

On one of my trips to the Solomons, I visited Malaita, the second-most-populous island after Guadalcanal, where the Solomons' capital, Honiara, is located. The only airport on the island did not have a hard-surface runway, and on my departure the main terminal was ankle-deep in water raining through holes in the roof. The local official I was there to interview met me in a ramshackle one-room office; he was barefoot and explained that he was never told what his duties were by anyone in the government. In the Solomons and in PNG, there were continual property-rights disputes where a foreign investor—often a mining or logging company—was seeking access to land. There had been repeated attempts to build a port in Malaita, but plans were being constantly held up by tribal leaders. In this kind of system, there were no individual Western-style property rights. Land was held collectively by a lineage, and each member had a say in its disposition, leading to very messy bargaining with hundreds of landowners.

I asked my driver about the status of the harbor negotiations. He was a heavyset, affable fellow who had grown up on Malaita. He said they were unlikely to come to an agreement anytime soon. I asked him whether his own ancestors were buried on the contested land for the port; he said they were, and that he could never agree to giving the foreign company the right to uproot their graves. Twenty years later, that harbor remains unbuilt.

These trips underlined to me the way in which Western institutions, such as alienable private property rights, were imposed on top of societies with very different social structures. They simply didn't work. Britain and then Australia, the former colonial masters, had bequeathed to PNG a Westminster-style parliamentary system, with a first-past-the-post electoral system in which the candidate with the plurality of votes won. This kind of voting system, used in Britain and the United States, tends to produce a two-party duopoly in the legislature, something political scientists label

"Duverger's Law." In PNG, there were no political parties organized around ideology or policy issues; rather, people voted for "big men" who were leaders of kinship groups. In every election, there would be dozens of candidates for a single seat, and the winner often had a vote share in the low single digits. This led to a huge amount of instability in parliament, since most members lost their narrow pluralities after just one election cycle.

In the early 2000s, PNG replaced their plurality system with preferential voting, or what we in the United States call "ranked choice" voting, where citizens vote for multiple candidates and rank order them. Many Americans think that this is too complicated a voting system for their fellow citizens to understand, but people in PNG—where the literacy rate is just over 60 percent—adjusted to it just fine after a couple of election cycles. This system may have increased the stability of parliament marginally, since candidates needed to come to agreements on their followers' second choices.

It is much better for institutions to evolve organically within societies. Those brought from the outside sometimes stick, such as the 1946 Japanese constitution, which was written by a small group of Americans. But more often than not, they become hollow shells that mask a very different social reality.

The other thing that I took away from my time in Melanesia was the importance of national identity. Papua New Guinea is famous for its fragmentation. Though humans have been living in the region for perhaps forty thousand years, PNG is home to nearly eight hundred mutually incomprehensible languages. The primary social unit is the *wontok*—a pidgin corruption of the English words "one talk"—which is spoken in a particular mountain valley. Members of a *wontok* don't feel they have much in common with their neighbors over the ridge line, and in fact violence among these small groups has been endemic for centuries. While I was there, there was a lot of opposition to a proposal to build a highway between the capital, Port Moresby, and Lae, the country's second-largest city, because the people in Moresby didn't want northerners coming down to their city.

Thus many parts of the Papuan interior are accessible only by plane. We flew up into the highlands on the Indonesian side of the island in a little four-seater aircraft from the city of Jayapura. There was a choice of airlines, a Protestant one and a Catholic one, operated by the two Christian sects as part of their missions. The mountain runway was very short and sloped; the pilot landed uphill and took off downhill. As we flew in to the airstrip we could see the wreckage of several planes that had crashed there in previous years.

We witnessed a meeting of big men designated by the Indonesian government as local officials. Some had had to walk for several days to get to the conference site; they all had clean uniforms and seemed better organized than their counterparts on the PNG side. One of the big men attending was naked except for a penis gourd, originating from somewhere around his groin, that must have been four feet long.

One could argue that Melanesia would be better off left to its own culture and traditions, without well-meaning outside efforts to promote growth and development. There are a number of problems with such an approach, however. The country's social statistics—under-five mortality, life expectancy, malnutrition, women dying in childbirth—are terrible. The other problem is that the outside world won't leave them alone. The rainforests in PNG are being despoiled by Malaysian and Chinese logging companies, and the ground torn up by huge foreign mining operations. The Solomon Islands have become a pawn in the China-Taiwan rivalry, with China having signed a mutual security agreement with Honiara in 2023 to woo it away from Taiwan.

The experience of these Melanesian societies demonstrates the need for a centralized state, but also the extraordinary difficulty in building one. Afghanistan and Iraq had experience of a state in earlier years—in Iraq's case, a state that was far too strong and tyrannical. These collapsed under US intervention and had to be reconstructed. PNG and the Solomons, by contrast, were stateless societies prior to their colonization by the European powers, and were building states from a much lower base. They were seeking to do in a couple of decades what had taken Western societies centuries to accomplish, and were not doing it particularly well.

30

ON DELEGATION

THE PROBLEM OF DELEGATING AUTHORITY IN AN ORGAnization may not seem like a pressing or even interesting issue, yet it has been one of my central preoccupations over recent years. I've come to see that it is the core of what is called "management" or administration, both private and public, and that it is the key to government effectiveness. In the year 2025 delegation has become a central issue in American politics as the Trump administration launches an assault on what it labels the "deep state," and is an important source of political polarization, even if many Americans don't realize that this is what they're fighting about.

Especially after the publication of my second book, *Trust*, I started getting invitations to speak at corporate events. Corporate executives love to talk about trust, and feel they can't get enough of it in their organizations. As I started to think about how to apply the idea of trust to a corporate hierarchy, it became clear that all organizations need to delegate authority, and that trust is critical to successful delegation.

Toyota had undercut the US auto industry in the 1970s and 1980s with its *kanban*, or just-in-time, system, in which inventories were kept very low and assembly-line workers could pull a cord at their workstations and stop the entire process if they saw a defect or problem. The point of the system was to create big incentives to eliminate mistakes and defects at the source, rather than in the rework areas at the end of the assembly line. Just-in-time in effect delegated huge power to low-level workers, and would only work if they could be trusted to pull the cord only when they saw a genuine problem. In a low-trust society with poisonous labor-management relations, as in many European countries in this period, the workers would have been pulling the cord all the time just to screw the managers. Trust was also central to Toyota's relationship with its suppliers. Under what was known as "relational contracting," large Japanese corporations such as Toyota would encourage the sharing of ideas with contractors and maintain long-term relationships even if the latter didn't offer the cheapest prices in the short run.

I thought at the time that I detected a similar difference between Ford and General Motors (GM), both of which had adopted just-in-time in their North American factories. GM saw this simply as a way of minimizing the cost of inventories, while Ford worked to develop good relations with the United Auto Workers (UAW) union and insisted that its suppliers do the same. When GM was hit with a couple of strikes in this period, the just-in-time system guaranteed that stoppages would immediately proliferate throughout its North American operations. Their vice president for supply chain management at the time, José Ignacio López, was a low-trust fellow famous for squeezing every last penny out of subcontractors, taking their intellectual property and forcing them to compete against one another.

Sometime in the late 1990s I was invited to Dearborn to speak to the Ford senior management, which included the company's CEO at the time, Jacques Nasser. I was very proud of my insight about just-in-time, and explained to the dinner crowd how they had made use of trust in their relationship with the UAW and how critical it was to efficiency.

You can quickly tell when a speech does not go over well. No one nods in response to things you say, and no one except the event organizer raises their hand in the Q&A session. The elevator ride down to the executive garage after dinner with a group of vice presidents, as they waited to get into their Jaguars, was excruciating. (It was at that point that I realized why Ford had purchased Jaguar in 1990—so that its executives wouldn't have to ride in Fords and Lincolns.) My theory had totally flopped.

This didn't necessarily mean the theory was wrong; it did indicate that Ford's management didn't fully understand the *kanban* system and why it promoted quality. They didn't see that trust between workers and managers increased the flow of information in the system, which then led to quality and productivity improvements.

My real confrontation with the issue of delegated authority came sometime after that, as I was working on the last study I did for the Rand Corporation.

In the years prior to the dot-com bust of 2001, management gurus were abuzz with ideas about flat management and decentralized authority. Silicon Valley's success in this heady period was said to lie in its adoption of highly distributed authority that flowed through networks rather than hierarchical systems. In those years, complexity theory and "spontaneous order" were very trendy, and everyone was flocking to the Santa Fe Institute to learn about "complex adaptive systems."

Economists began to recognize the importance of hierarchies in the 1930s with the publication of a paper by Ronald Coase at the University of Chicago entitled "The Nature of the Firm." Coase asked why vertically integrated companies such as Ford or General Motors existed. If decentralized market transactions were so much more efficient than central planning, he wondered, why was the American economy organized around gigantic corporations allocating resources by administrative fiat? One could imagine a car being created in a decentralized and outsourced manner, with separate companies designing, fabricating, and marketing the final product. Instead, the big auto companies did everything from mining iron ore and producing steel to designing cars and selling them through networks of dealerships they controlled. Why did they exercise such centralized authority?

The answer, Coase said, was transaction costs: it would take too much time and effort for separate companies to coordinate the building of a car, with contracting, lawyers, negotiations, and litigation at every stage. It was much more efficient to do this through an administrative hierarchy, in which a central body could simply dictate goals and order different parts of the company to work together. In capitalist economies, large companies were organized as if they were mini socialist systems.

Coase's insights became very central with the rise of the internet and the popularity of neoliberalism in the 1990s. The kind of market economics promoted at Coase's University of Chicago sought to minimize state intervention, and emphasized possibilities for the emergence of order without hierarchy. Some economists, such as Thomas Malone, began to speculate that this new thing called the internet would create a third zone of "networks" between markets and hierarchies, because it would dramatically reduce transaction costs and make horizontal coordination much easier. At the same time, there was rising interest in what were called "complex adaptive systems," in which order was created not by a hierarchy giving orders but through spontaneous "emergent" behaviors undertaken by individual actors. The apparent order in a flock of birds did not come about because there was a lead bird directing his fellows where to fly; rather, it emerged as a result of each member of the flock following relatively simple behavioral rules such as "turn when the bird next to you turns."

The antiauthoritarian zeitgeist of the 1990s led to some amusing results. In one experiment, a large group of people in a movie theater were asked to collectively fly a simulated airplane by voting on its direction with individual buttons. Needless to say, this worked a lot less well than flying the plane with a single experienced pilot. Anyone who has sat in endless committee meetings where decisions need to be taken by consensus understands why there are limits to the "wisdom of crowds."

As the dot-com bubble burst at the beginning of the twenty-first century, it was clear that the internet was not going to undercut the need for hierarchy. Vertical structures of authority came to be understood by economists in terms of what they called "principal-agent" theory, which became the dominant paradigm for understanding phenomena such as corruption. At the top of the hierarchy stood the principal, who issued mandates to various layers of agents who were to carry them out. Corruption occurred when the agents sought their own advantage rather than carrying out the wishes of the principal. Corruption could be minimized by aligning the incentives of the agents with those of the principal; this was the justification for the widespread use of stock options as a form of compensation in Silicon Valley. Employees of the firm would presumably be motivated to seek the good of the firm as a whole rather than focus on their own salaries and careers.

But while principal-agent may have been a useful initial cut at how to think about hierarchical relationships, it often didn't correspond to reality. Herbert Simon, another economics Nobel Prize winner, noted that authority often flowed not from top to bottom but rather from bottom to top in many organizations. This was because the frontline workers at the bottom of the hierarchy often had more knowledge about the actual situation they faced, and more expertise in how to solve problems.

This was a point that had been made in an important 1945 article by Friedrich Hayek, the godfather of libertarian economists, called "The Use of Knowledge in Society." Hayek, who was at that point in a famous debate with Joseph Schumpeter on the relative merits of markets versus central planning, noted that the vast majority of information in an economy was local in nature. If you were bolting on a door panel to a chassis in an auto plant and the hinges didn't align properly, it was the assembly-line worker and not a corporate vice president who understood the problem. This suggested that while hierarchies were necessary for high-level coordination, they would need to delegate significant authority to low-level workers who possessed local knowledge. Hayek concluded from this that market economies would necessarily be more efficient than centrally planned ones.

The genius of the Toyota *kanban* system was not its minimizing of inventories but its delegation of authority over quality control to frontline workers.

Libertarians such as Hayek wanted to believe that society could be organized through the voluntary cooperation of individuals, while socialists and corporate bosses believed that centralized control was necessary. From this evolving discussion I drew the conclusion that they were both to some extent right: you couldn't do away with the need for hierarchy, but within a hierarchy it was necessary to delegate as much authority as possible to lower-level agents with knowledge and skills, who could be trusted to collaborate to solve problems. I came to understand that *the* central problem in all organizations, and therefore of politics as a whole, was that of "delegated discretion": how much and what sorts of authority should be delegated to bureaucratic agents in a hierarchical system.

It was against this background that my old friend Abe Shulsky and I undertook a study at the Rand Corporation for the US Army Training and Doctrine Command (TRADOC) on whether some of these flat management ideas from Silicon Valley could be applied to the US military. We went around to various army bases and training centers, including a stop at the XVIII Airborne Corps headquarters at Fort Bragg, North Carolina. (This is where I first met David Petraeus, who as a battalion commander had just jumped out of an airplane in an overnight training exercise.) As we talked to officers and read more deeply into the literature, we came to realize that the army already practiced a form of flat management, and that Silicon Valley had absolutely nothing to teach it in this regard.

The US military had done very poorly in Vietnam, operating under a rigid command structure in which decisions were made by higher-ups, going all the way up to the president in some cases. Following the US withdrawal in the early 1970s, the army engaged in a prolonged lessons-learned exercise, in which it reevaluated the doctrines that had led to these results.

This review led to the adoption by the 1980s of the army's own form of flat management under the heading of "mission orders" or "commander's intent." The new doctrine said that the maximum amount of authority should be delegated to the lowest possible level in the command structure. It was the second lieutenant trying to assault a building, and not a general hundreds of kilometers behind the front lines, who had the best understanding of the tactical situation. The generals were there to make only the higher-level strategic and operational decisions, leaving implementation of their orders up to junior officers. That lieutenant was the equivalent of the assembly-line worker at Toyota who knew more about production problems than the vice president sitting in corporate headquarters.

"Mission orders" was rooted in the German doctrine of *Auftragstaktik*, which had first emerged at the end of World War I to guide the new storm trooper battalions. It had become institutionalized by the time of the Second World War and incorporated into the operations of the Panzer divisions that conquered France. Local commanders were given the autonomy to make decisions on their own without having to refer them to higher headquarters. This kind of delegated authority worked well against the rigid, centralized command structures of many older armies. It was adopted wholeheartedly by the Israeli Defense Forces and was one of the reasons why the IDF outfought its Arab opponents in the wars of 1956, 1967, and, after some initial setbacks, 1973. It is one of the reasons that the Ukrainian army, after the 2022 full-scale Russian invasion, did so well against its much larger opponent. Russia, like the Soviet Union before it, has tended to rely on mass and firepower within a rigid, centralized command structure.

Abe Shulsky and I published our findings in a Rand report that came out in 1997. Ever since then, I've been acutely aware of the centrality and ultimate difficulty of determining what constitutes the proper level of delegation. No large organization can function without delegating substantial authority to lower echelons of its hierarchy. Yet delegating means giving up control, and the subordinate agents can make decisions that are at cross-purposes with what the principal wants. The venerable Barings Bank was brought down in 1995 when a young trader named Nick Leeson was given the authority to in effect "bet the firm."

The economists who came up with principal-agent theory—the framework most typically used to study problems such as corruption—assume that the principal is always right and that organizational dysfunction lies in the agent not doing what the boss wants. But strict principal control over agents doesn't always produce good outcomes. In many cases the agent has more expertise than the principal, and understands better how to accomplish the principal's objectives. In other cases it is the principal who is ordering the agent to do things that are unethical, corrupt, or illegal. In these circumstances, agent autonomy—that is, the agent's ability to evade the principal's orders—actually constitutes an important check on abuses of executive power.

Delegation has become a huge issue in American politics. Conservatives have been complaining about the "administrative state" ever since the massive expansion of the federal government during the New Deal in the 1930s. With the rise of Donald Trump, they have been vowing to destroy the "deep state." They complain about the ability of "unelected bureaucrats" to block or slow-walk presidential policies they don't favor, and to push their own favored left-leaning policies. During the early months of the Trump administration, the billionaire Elon Musk was given control of a Department of Government Efficiency (DOGE) and allowed to randomly destroy parts of the US government.

Much of the field of administrative law revolves around the question of what degree of delegation is permitted by the Constitution, and how political authorities may legitimately control the behavior of their subordinates. Today in American politics there is a huge distrust of expertise and unwillingness to accept many established sources of authority. In 2024 a conservative Supreme Court invalidated the 1984 Chevron deference decision that delegated authority to the expertise of agencies.

The conservative narrative about the tyranny of unelected bureaucrats that the United States is allegedly living under gets things 180 degrees wrong. The problem with the US bureaucracy is not that it has too much power, but that it has too little. For example, every federal agency is encumbered by the Federal Acquisition Regulation (the FAR), thousands of pages of rules governing how they are to procure equipment and adjudicate disputes. This is why government procurement is so slow and more expensive than in the private sector. Equally complex personnel rules explain why it takes nine months to hire an entry-level federal employee.

All liberal democracies face a crisis of governance today, where they are not able to deliver the outcomes desired by their citizens. In addition to national-level regulations, the European Union has created an impenetrable mass of rules in its *acquis communautaire*. American government suffers from similar overregulation at state and federal levels, driven by a deep-seated distrust of government. The solution to this problem is not to add further layers of rules to control the behavior of bureaucrats; rather, they ought to be given more freedom to exercise judgment and common sense in implementing policies set by their political masters. Civilian agencies need to adopt more of the spirit of "mission orders" that governs military organizations.

Bureaucracy is the way we guarantee airline safety, approve the safety of food and drugs, manage the money supply, and provide Social Security checks to retirees. Rather than being further restricted in their autonomy by the piling on of yet more rules, bureaucrats need to be given greater authority to use their own judgment in making decisions and delivering services to citizens. Yet that bureaucracy is today demonized, distrusted, and in line to be dismantled by people operating on a false narrative who do not know what they are doing.

31

AI AND THE PROBLEM OF DELEGATION

WHILE DELEGATION OF AUTHORITY TO "UNELECTED bureaucrats" in the American bureaucracy is a red herring, it will definitely become a problem as artificial intelligence continues to spread.

There are two types of fears regarding artificial intelligence. The first is short-run and materializing before our eyes: AI can be used by bad people to do bad things, such as manipulate voters, break into bank accounts, undermine trust in media and institutions, and the like. Deep fakes are now a routine part of what we see online.

There is another, more apocalyptic fear engendered by AI, however, which worries that the technology poses an existential risk to mankind as a whole. While malevolent, out-of-control robots have long been part of science fiction, it has been hard to understand exactly how this might come about. A potential pathway is becoming clear, however: it lies through "agentic" AI, and the threat will arise due to the very high likelihood that we will delegate too much control to AI agents.

Agentic AI is already here in a variety of forms. There are many programs running in the background—in Linux systems, they are called "daemons"—that continuously monitor things such as the state of your computer. Other AI agents watch environmental conditions, the appearance of intruders, and the like, and are authorized to take action without being given explicit permission by a human being.

As AI agents become increasingly capable, we will want to delegate more authority to them. This will happen for the same reason that it is necessary for existing organizations to delegate substantial authority to low-level human agents: those agents are often more knowledgeable and have skills that their principals don't have, and can react much more quickly to local conditions.

We see this happening already in military affairs. Drones are being heavily used in the Russia-Ukraine war, and are now equipped with AI capabilities to pick out targets. While governments try to insist on keeping a "human in the loop" before issuing a potentially lethal order, this check is being eroded through sheer battlefield necessity. Agentic AI software on a military drone can understand its immediate environment and react to threats much more quickly than one controlled by a human being, and the penalty for not delegating lethal authority may itself be lethal to the drone's masters.

There has been a lot of speculation as to if and when a machine will achieve artificial general intelligence (AGI); that is, intelligence as good as or better than that of a human being, or beyond that, superintelligence. We don't need to speculate about this; we can, however, know with certainty that AI agents will become much more capable in the not-so-distant future and will be able to make a host of decisions autonomously. "Loss of control" has become a major theme in AI research, and there has been a lot of speculation about ways that a highly intelligent and capable AI agent might cover its own tracks and escape the notice of its human creators. What is worrisome is that a lot of the capabilities of sophisticated AIs are "emergent," meaning that they were not deliberately programmed into the machine but arose unexpectedly from its underlying capabilities. Today's most advanced AIs are not being programmed by human beings as computers were previously; they are described instead as "growing" because they program themselves.

One of the big issues in any form of delegation is the matter of trust. While principals can impose a number of external controls on their agents and monitor their actions, in the end they need to be able to trust the good judgment and loyalty of the agents themselves. Human beings have evolved complex faculties for making judgments about the trustworthiness of other human beings, but we may not know how to evaluate the trustworthiness of a machine that has programmed itself.

This does not necessarily spell disaster for the human race, but it does mean that the problem of delegation will only grow more acute as technology advances.

32

VETOCRACY

WHILE LIBERAL DEMOCRACY MAY IN PRINCIPLE BE THE best form of government, there are many different ways to organize such a political system, and some work better than others. Political institutions need to be tailored to the particular societies in which they exist, as any comparative political scientist will tell you. For example, federalism (the delegation of authority to lower levels of government) is typically more necessary in large, diverse countries such as Brazil, India, or the United States, than it is in smaller, more homogeneous ones such as the Netherlands or Israel. Furthermore, both institutions and their underlying societies evolve. *Political Order and Political Decay* told the story of how institutions became rigid over time and failed to adapt to social change, particularly change brought on by economic modernization. Alternatively, states could be "captured" by powerful elites within their societies, who would pervert political power to serve their own narrow interests.

All political systems seek to generate and use power; liberal democracies also aim to constrain that power under a rule of law and democratic accountability. Governments can be too strong when rulers accumulate power with few constraints, but they can also be too weak when they are blocked from exercising legitimate power by other social actors, from overly powerful interest groups to narco-trafficking gangs or foreign powers. The best governments are ones that have adequate power to provide things that citizens want, such as security, economic growth, education, and health care, while not abusing that power to take away the rights of individuals or unduly dominate the society they rule.

Americans are primed to focus on the threat of excessive government power. As a result, they have erected many different barriers to the exercise of state power, something we refer to as checks and balances. We typically think that such checks are a good thing, and that the more there are, the better. Americans spread power out by having, in contrast to a parliamentary system, a separately elected president in addition to the legislature, with equal democratic legitimacy; they have a powerful upper house, the Senate, that in contrast to many other democracies is needed to pass legislation and has reserved powers on cabinet and judicial appointments; they devolve power to states, counties, and municipalities in a complex system of federalism; and they have a Supreme Court that can invalidate ordinary legislation on constitutional grounds. Many of these checks are then replicated on a state level. Moreover, there are nonconstitutional checks on power, such as the filibuster rule in the Senate that allows a minority of forty-one out of a hundred senators to block legislation they don't like.

This complex system should be contrasted with other liberal democracies with fewer checks and balances. The classic British Westminster system, for example, has no federalism, no separate presidency, no powerful upper house, no powerful Supreme Court, and indeed no written constitution that can define the limits of executive authority. A simple majority of 50 percent plus one member of Parliament is sufficient to pass legislation. Britain, like the United States, has a plurality or "first past the post" voting system where the winner in a single district is the candidate with the largest number of votes, even if his or her vote share doesn't constitute a majority of voters. The consequence is that parliamentary majorities are often created by a minority of citizens. A British Parliament could in theory take away basic rights of citizens, such as freedom of speech, with a simple majority vote. The only real check on Parliament's power is the threat of losing the next election.

While the British Westminster system is a bit extreme in the way it concentrates power, the United States stands at the other end of the spectrum: no other modern liberal democracy has as many checks and balances as the United States. Indeed, when that system is combined with a highly polarized electorate, as it has been for the past couple of decades, the result is pervasive gridlock and the inability to make decisions on a host of important policy issues. This is reflected in the periodic shutdowns of the US government due to a failure of Congress to pass an annual budget, one of the most basic functions of any modern government. Many other issues, such as comprehensive immigration reform, gun control, and reform of the electoral process, have not been addressed despite evidence that a majority of Americans would support compromise outcomes.

In the second volume of my *Political Order* series I coined the term "vetocracy" to describe what the American political system has become. Checks and balances are of course critical for the proper functioning of any democracy that hopes to be liberal at the same time. Donald Trump in his first term chafed at the constraints placed on him to do things he wanted to do, such as banning Muslims from entering the country, building a border wall to keep out immigrants, or using the Justice Department to go after political enemies. In his second term in office, he has vowed not to be similarly constrained, and has been routinely disobeying laws and rules meant to check the president's power.

While checks and balances may help to prevent abuses of power, they also prevent good things from happening. And in a curious way, the failure to use power legitimately fuels the desire to use power illegitimately.

This can be seen in the realm of law enforcement. Criminal defendants in the United States have a host of legal protections, beginning with the Miranda rights that all policemen need to read to them when they are arrested. There are huge procedural obstacles to bringing offenders to justice, in a process that is both time-consuming and slow. One of the results of this is a popular culture that celebrates vigilante justice, where a film's protagonist is celebrated for taking the law into his or her own hands and gunning down an evildoer that the legal system could not hold accountable. Strongmen in other countries such as Rodrigo Duterte in the Philippines and Nayib Bukele in El Salvador have been celebrated on the right for their willingness to use extrajudicial measures against criminals and gang members. Going around the law has become a staple of Donald Trump's repertoire; he has recommended shooting shoplifters or protestors in the legs, using uncontrolled police violence to intimidate criminals, and using the US military to sink boats in international waters that his administration believes are guilty of smuggling drugs.

Vetocracy in the United States is responsible for the country's failure to build things. In 2010, I moved to California, a state dominated by the Democratic Party, which is famous for the myriad of obstacles it puts in the way of infrastructure projects. The United States, virtually alone among modern liberal democracies, does not enforce its own laws in many domains. It is left up to private citizens to file lawsuits against perceived wrongdoers in a practice referred to as "private right of action," or private attorney generals. This is true of a good deal of environmental law. The State of California passed the California Environmental Quality Act (CEQA) back in 1970, giving all of the state's nearly 40 million residents standing to sue any project they believe is harming the environment. They can do this anonymously and with no statute of limitations. Only a small minority of CEQA lawsuits have been filed by environmental organizations. The rest are filed by NIMBY ("not in my backyard") neighbors, business competitors, or labor unions that want to force contractors to hire unionized workers. Because CEQA is a useful tool for legal extortion, it has proven impossible for a series of governors to repeal or modify. CEQA means that there are 40 million potential veto points in California, and explains why a high-speed rail system that would have cost about $20 billion to build in China is likely to cost well over $100 billion in the Golden State. The truth of the matter is that high-speed rail is very unlikely to ever be constructed.

Californians love to tell CEQA horror stories. Take the case of the 710 Freeway. Back in the late 1960s, the state bought the right-of-way for a four-mile stretch of freeway that would connect the Ports of Long Beach and Los Angeles to Interstate 5 and the larger freeway network in Southern California. Those ports host the largest container terminals on the West Coast of the United States, and are critical to the movement of trade from East Asia and Latin America.

The proposed extension ran through the city of South Pasadena, however, and when CEQA passed in 1971, the city sued to block it as an environmental hazard. A local judge upheld their suit and the freeway was blocked. Virtually every governor of California over the subsequent fifty years has tried to move the project forward, and none has succeeded. In a more recent case, the University of California, Berkeley, wanted to admit an additional three thousand students to its campus, in an era where competition to get into elite schools was intense. The upper-middle-class neighbors of the school sued under CEQA, claiming that the extra students would in effect constitute a pollutant that would degrade the quality of the environment in their neighborhood. So the dormitories were blocked. In terms of their own agenda, it is one thing for environmentalists to block a big shopping mall or high-end condo in order to preserve a middle-class neighborhood; quite another to stop offshore wind farms or transmission lines that are necessary to meet carbon emission targets in an age of global warming.

The story of vetocracy is not limited to California, or the United States. There was a European vision to build a high-speed railway all the way from Paris to Vienna, with a node at the southwestern German city of Stuttgart. Plans were first made in the late 1980s before German unification, and ground was first broken during the late 1990s. But all modern infrastructure projects require extensive consultation with citizens, and the German planners failed to undertake this properly. When bulldozers came to rip up the plane trees near the old station in the middle of the city, high school students protested by chaining themselves to the trees. The conflict escalated, to the point where the Christian Democrats who had been governing the state of Baden-Württemberg since the founding of the Federal Republic in 1949 were unseated by a Red-Green coalition. The station remains unfinished to the present day. The problem of vetocracy seems endemic to modern liberal democracies.

Frustration with vetocracy then breeds its opposite, an authoritarian impulse to set aside the rule of law altogether and simply get things done by force of will. This is where Donald Trump's rule by executive order comes from, and how Nayib Bukele gets reelected with a huge vote share after having locked up a significant percentage of El Salvador's young male population. What is missing is an understanding of the rule of law that sees state power as a potentially beneficial force that can achieve public purposes without undermining individual rights. Democracies need to be able to build things.

33

LEARNING TO LOVE BUREAUCRATS

IF THIS HAS NOT BEEN MADE SUFFICIENTLY CLEAR IN the preceding sections, there is a clear line of thought that ties together the things I have written and done over the past twenty years. That thread begins with the September 11 attacks and leads eventually to the importance of protecting the American bureaucracy from Donald Trump and his administration, which wants to dismantle the "deep state."

The US occupations of Afghanistan and Iraq demonstrated more clearly than any academic study the importance of having a functioning state that possesses a legitimate monopoly of force. My visits to Melanesia underlined the consequences of statelessness, but also the coherence of tribal societies as an alternative. The legitimacy of their old ways of life was weakened, but they were nowhere close to creating functional modern states in their place. My time in Latin America reinforced a different point. Mexico, Colombia, Peru, and many other countries in the region suffered from state weakness that permitted the proliferation of crime and narco-trafficking, and held back their prospects for either economic growth or stable democracy.

Central to my thinking about the good functioning of modern governments is the problem of delegation. Any organization, and particularly large ones like governments, has to delegate authority. The logic of this lies in Friedrich Hayek's 1945 article on local knowledge: it is the people at the bottom of the hierarchy and not those at the top who often have the local knowledge and skills to make good decisions. If those workers are given sufficient authority, they can also make decisions much faster than in systems where authority has to travel up and down a long chain of command. This is why all good militaries delegate as much responsibility as possible to junior officers. This is just the military version of bureaucratic autonomy, which needs to be practiced in civilian organizations as well.

But principals can't delegate to agents unless they trust those agents. Trust arises from a number of sources. Primary among them, especially in a complex, high-tech society, is professionalism, education, and technical skills that allow low-level workers to make good decisions without constantly referring them to those at the top. Training and education—what we call "capacity"—are therefore critical.

But there is a moral dimension as well. Workers have to be governed by norms that allow them to cooperate flexibly with their fellows. These norms can come from a variety of sources: shared religion or culture, common education, or simply the experience of working together at a common task over a period of time. Often, it is the most difficult and dangerous tasks that bind people the most strongly, which is why soldiers in small units are willing to risk their lives for their fellows. It is possible to get people to cooperate using a system of formal rules, which becomes more necessary as the scale of the organization increases. But the most efficient systems rely on internalized informal norms that act like a lubricant facilitating cooperation. This is what I label "social capital."

Social capital differs from one society to the next, and between different groups in the same society. It may arise from long-standing shared cultural practices, but it can also arise as the result of deliberate actions or institutions that cultivate shared norms within a group. This is why good leadership remains important regardless of how well institutionalized an organization is: leaders are the ones who create shared norms and culture through their own example.

Among rich liberal democracies, the United States has always had serious problems with delegation. The United States was born in a revolution against monarchical authority, in which distrust of government was endemic. Therefore Americans from the beginning created a complex system of checks and balances that sought to limit the ability of the state to violate the rights of individuals. In many modern democracies, citizens regard the government as a benign institution that protects them from criminals, fraudsters, uncontrolled market forces, and foreign enemies. In the United States, people are more likely to see the government itself as the chief threat to their liberties.

The shared distrust of government has led Congress over the years to create a welter of rules and controls to oversee the behavior of state officials. Progressives in particular saw legitimacy residing in procedures, which they piled on even as they sought to make the government do more. But conservatives were also happy with new rules to slow the actions of government. This was what gave rise to vetocracy.

Bureaucratic dysfunction became a self-fulfilling prophecy, in which efforts to control the government made it less and less effective, and provoked calls for even more rules.

Modern states—states that treat citizens impersonally, are staffed by well-trained professionals, and are accountable to democratic publics—are therefore inherently fragile. Human nature here becomes a problem: human beings are inherently social creatures, and their sociability begins with loyalty to friends and family. At the center of the great struggles to create modern states out of patrimonial ones lies the exit from kinship. There were many ways of doing this: eunuchs were used in many imperial courts precisely because they supposedly couldn't have children; prefects and representatives of central governments could not hail from the territories over which they had authority, and were prevented from putting down roots there; and in the most extreme case, the Ottoman system of military slavery, young boys were torn from their families in foreign countries and made to serve the sultan as administrators and soldiers. The most durable system for building impersonal government was the examination system created in China, which built the first meritocracy more than two millennia ago and which is still in use today.

But the human preference for friends and family is so strong that repatrimonialization remains a constant threat to any modern political system. This form of political decay occurred historically in China, Turkey, and France, and is happening today in the United States as a new administration seeks to staff the US government with friends and family.

Thus winds the thread that started with the failure of the Afghan and Iraqi states and led eventually to the present crisis in American government.

34

THE LONG MARCH THROUGH INSTITUTIONS

HAVING STARTED OUT IN THE HUMANITIES, I MADE several gradual turns toward subjects that were less abstract and high-level, toward those more oriented to the practicalities of living in the world. This began with a switch from comparative literature and classics to political science, and has led me to an agenda for teaching and work over the past couple of decades.

I've spent most of my career in public policy institutions: the Rand Corporation, George Mason's Institute of Public Policy (now the Schar School of Policy and Government), the Rand School of Public Policy, and the Johns Hopkins School of Advanced International Studies (SAIS).

I came to Stanford in 2010 to work at the Center on Democracy, Development and the Rule of Law, which is part of the Freeman Spogli Institute for International Studies (FSI), an interdisciplinary research institute. My center has studied problems of democracy internationally, though with the rise of Trump and his populist movement after 2015, there has been an increasing focus on American politics. Unlike Stanford's academic departments, FSI's research has been focused on international policy issues.

My two experiences working in the State Department, as well as a lifetime of observing the workings of the US government, convinced me that the teaching of public policy in the United States was woefully inadequate. Like many other disciplines, the field of public policy has been colonized by the economists for several decades now. Students are taught a range of quantitative skills; they learn how to apply econometric techniques to datasets to establish causal relationships, such as those between classroom size and test outcomes, or how to incentivize the uptake of mosquito bed nets in poor countries. All of this is done in the interest of improving the effectiveness of public policies.

Political prestige lies in being a policymaker; for example, the person who rolls out a prison reform program or a new way of subsiding calorie intake in Bangladesh. Being a policymaker is regarded as serious work; being the person who actually implements the policy out in the real world has much less social status.

The problem is that the "real world" is full of obstacles and constraints that prevent seemingly optimal policies from actually being carried out. Policymakers seldom think about these constraints when designing their policies, and then are disappointed to discover that the policies don't get done. They are not taught in school about things like Washington's "interagency process," around which policy implementation revolves. Moreover, they tend not to talk to the citizens who will be affected by those policies—for example, to find out whether they really want a new train station in the middle of the old city, or how to get past the criminal gangs who are preventing the distribution of water from the municipal water system. Many programs touted by politicians in the United States have failed, because the policymakers didn't realize that the website for signing up for benefits is unusable unless you have the latest version of Adobe Acrobat on your phone. Economists have been explaining for years that the most efficient way to reduce carbon emissions is to impose a uniform carbon tax. The only problem is that one of the two major political parties has put it in their party's platform that they will never accept such a tax, and indeed want to continue to subsidize gas and oil.

These kinds of problems are particularly evident when trying to carry out a major infrastructure project. Such projects are meant to provide what economists call "public goods," meaning things of general benefit to the community, such as electricity, clean water, or efficient public transportation. But building such things always hurts some individual's private interest—their land must be claimed, they'll lose their nice view of the ocean, or their neighborhood will lose its suburban character. Completion of these kinds of projects thus requires not simply technical engineering knowledge or an economist's cost-benefit analysis, but also political skills in learning how to bring stakeholders along.

Such considerations are what led me and a colleague from SAIS, Roger Leeds, to establish something we called the Leadership Academy for Development at Stanford back in 2009. The community of people and institutions that sought to promote development in poor countries had at that point given up on the Washington Consensus, the series of liberalizing reforms that had been dominant since the Reagan-Thatcher era. With the rise of what was called the New Institutional Economics, economists began to take politics seriously and realized that growth would not be possible in countries plagued by insecurity, corruption, or weak governments unable to provide basic public goods for their citizens. Instead of trying to get the state out of the management of the economy, economists turned their focus to issues such as building the capacity of states to do positive things and to reduce corruption.

When Roger and I thought about how we could contribute to this "good governance" agenda, we decided that since we were educators, the optimal path would be to teach up-and-coming leaders in developing countries about the importance of implementation and its relationship to policy design. Thus was born the Leadership Academy for Development, and a framework for solving public policy problems that could be taught in an intensive one-week program. Over the years our framework evolved, and I and Jeremy Weinstein—a political scientist who is now the dean of the Harvard Kennedy School of Government—incorporated it into the international public policy master's program that I began directing at Stanford.

We've offered dozens of these Leadership Academy programs all over the world over the past decade and a half, and this has kept me on airplanes continually in recent years. Our geographical focus shifted over the years, and especially after the Russian seizure of Crimea in 2014, we focused heavily on parts of the former Soviet Union such as the Republic of Georgia and Ukraine. This is one of the reasons I took Vladimir Putin's full-scale invasion of Ukraine in 2022 so personally. Ukraine is full of well-educated young people who want to leave behind the Soviet legacy, with its corrupt, authoritarian politics, and become part of Europe. For them, the "West" embodies personal and political freedom, uncorrupt government, and economic growth, and they don't want to be sucked back into Putin's project of re-creating a twenty-first-century version of the USSR.

At the present moment, there are radicals who are seeking shortcuts to a better society. They are most prominent on the right, where Donald Trump's most impassioned supporters vow to destroy the "deep state." Like all historical revolutionaries, they have no idea how to create new, better institutions to replace those they believe are corrupt and oppressive. There is a similar impulse on the progressive left, which also has a jaundiced view of the existing political system but no clear vision of how it should be replaced. Both groups believe that they can somehow leapfrog the slow process of institution-building and get to a better life by tearing down what exists at present.

It was the Marxist theorist Antonio Gramsci who offered the most sensible advice to young radicals. They had to make the "long march through institutions" if they were to achieve power and accomplish their goals. This long march takes you through democratic politics: mobilizing, arguing, debating, and ultimately winning elections. And after the election, it leads you to public policy—not just designing the systems that you believe will make people's lives better, but thinking through how to implement them in the real world. It's boring and slow, but this is how progress is made.

There are no shortcuts.

35

IN THE REALM OF THE LAST MAN

AS NOTED IN THE PREFACE, MANY CASUAL CRITICS OF the idea of "the end of history" failed to read what I had written beyond the title, and in particular paid no attention to the last five chapters of *The End of History and the Last Man*. Those chapters contain a clear premonition of the rise of the kind of demagogic populism that we have experienced from the mid-2010s to the present, a rise that threatens the stability of democracy in its metropole, the United States.

Kojève's Hegel departed from the real Hegel in the former's emphasis on the centrality of recognition as a driving force in human history. Kojève in fact saw the entire human historical process as a struggle for recognition, beginning with a "bloody battle" for "pure prestige." In *The End of History and the Last Man* I linked Hegelian recognition to Plato's discussion of *thymos* as a constituent part of the human soul. *Thymos* is the seat of pride because it is based on feelings of one's own worth or dignity, or what we today inadequately label "self-esteem." It also becomes the source of anger because it is the part that craves *recognition*: if we do not receive recognition of our dignity to the extent we believe we deserve, we become angry and often belligerent. *Thymos* reappears in almost all my books as a critical aspect both of human psychology and of human politics.

Kojève's great insight was that the demand for recognition was one of the fundamental drivers of human history, but also that the problem of unequal recognition—the master-slave dialectic—could only be resolved in a society based on mutual and equal recognition. In practical terms, this means creation of a liberal society that provides universal recognition by granting citizens equal rights: the rights to speak, to associate, to believe, and to have a share of political power through the vote.

The process of making equal recognition a reality is one that is far from being fully realized. But it is utterly foolish to believe that *no* progress has been made toward this end since 1789, when the Constitution was ratified, or 1620, when slavery came to North America, or whatever other historical date one picks. The late twentieth century saw powerful social movements for civil rights, feminism, and LGBTQ rights that wiped away many of the formal legal barriers to de jure political equality, both in the United States and around the world.

The United States and its fellow liberal democracies in Europe and Asia are as politically free and materially prosperous as at any time in human history. Our problems are ones of extraordinary affluence, rather than material deprivation or gross injustice. Precisely because we have made such progress in previous decades, our expectations have grown much faster than our ability to solve our remaining problems, and have spawned radicalisms on both the extreme right and left that assert that things have never been worse than they are today.

Our very success raises the problem that I discussed in those seldom-read final chapters of my first book, the problem of the "Last Man."

The Last Man was the contemptuous phrase of Friedrich Nietzsche describing the kind of person who emerges at the end of history. The "Last Man" is a creature without pride or a striving to be something better, content with petty pleasures and material well-being. Kojève had defined the specifically human as the willingness to risk one's biological life for a cause, a form of freedom that no other "natural" creature possesses. But the very success of liberal societies produced peace and prosperity at a scale never before achieved in human history, and thereby took away the need for personal risk. The Last Men welcomed this; in Nietzsche's words, "and they blinked" like cattle.

Herein lies the potential for instability in successful liberal societies. All people want recognition of their equal dignity, something I labeled *isothymia*. From the French Revolution to the color revolutions of the early 2000s, this has been what has driven the struggle against dictatorship. But it turns out that not everyone is content to live in a state of peace and prosperity where they are recognized as the equal of every other human being on earth. They don't want to be a "Last Man," because this means becoming something less than human. Being a human with equal rights is not enough for many people; they want to be recognized as being superior.

This striving for superior respect is what I labeled *megalothymia*. This aspiration is an attribute, of course, of narcissists and tyrants. But *megalothymia* is also a necessary motivator of any kind of human excellence, from being a champion football forward to a rock star to a beloved novelist to an inspiring political leader. It is also the condition for the achievement of any form of social justice, since social movements need leaders and thrive on indignation at mistreatment of the marginalized. Certain human beings, in other words, are not content to be Last Men (or Last Women); they want to struggle to have their dignity recognized, or to have the dignity of other mistreated people acknowledged. If they are privileged to be living in an established, wealthy liberal democracy like that in the United States or those in Europe, they will turn against their own institutions. As I wrote back in 1992:

> Experience suggests that if men cannot struggle on behalf of a just cause because that just cause was victorious in an earlier generation, then they will struggle *against* the just cause. They will struggle for the sake of struggle. They will struggle, in other words, out of a certain boredom: for they cannot imagine living in a world without struggle. And if the greater part of the world in which they live is characterized by peaceful and prosperous liberal democracy, they then will struggle *against* that peace and prosperity, and against democracy.

Struggle for struggle's sake is what happens when we are at the end of history, when the world is actually in pretty good shape, and there are no great causes worthy of risking one's life.

We see this today on both the extreme right and left. The discontent on the right is more prominent, and has been driving the rise of populist movements all over the developed world. It is a reprise of a critique of liberalism made in the years prior to World War II. Leo Strauss gave a lecture on "German nihilism" in 1941 at the New School in New York that captured the essence of this vision. According to Strauss, what many young Germans hated in his day was the kind of society where people are content with peace and prosperity, where there is no striving for anything greater than physical comfort, where liberal tolerance forces everyone to be nonjudgmental, and where language itself is perverted in the interest of not offending the dignity of any group or individual in the society.

Liberal societies strive to be "nonjudgmental." But moral judgment is, according to Strauss, the core of what it means to be human. Strauss asked what the motive underlying the "protest against modern civilisation, against the spirit of the West, and in particular of the Anglo-Saxon West" was. He noted:

> The answer must be: it is a moral protest. That protest proceeds from the conviction that the internationalism inherent in modern civilisation, or, more precisely, that the establishment of a perfectly open society which is as it were the goal of modern civilisation, and therefore all aspirations directed toward that goal, are irreconcilable with the basic demands of moral life. That protest proceeds from the conviction that the root of all moral life is essentially and therefore eternally the closed society; from the conviction that the open society is bound to be, if not immoral, at least amoral: the meeting ground of seekers of pleasure, of gain, of irresponsible power, indeed of any kind of irresponsibility and lack of seriousness. Moral life, it is asserted, means serious life. Seri-

> ousness, and the ceremonial of seriousness—the flag and the oath to the flag—are the distinctive features of the closed society, of the society which by its very nature, is constantly confronted with, and basically oriented toward, the *Ernstfall*, the serious moment, M-day, war. Only life in such a tense atmosphere, only a life which is based on constant awareness of the sacrifices to which it owes its existence, and of the necessity, the duty of sacrifice of life and all worldly goods, is truly human: the sublime is unknown to the open society.

Put in somewhat different terms, a liberal society does not demand that we risk our lives on its behalf. Strauss points out that this does not necessarily imply militarism, but rather that there should be moral causes for which individuals are willing to risk their lives. We might recall that in Kojève's interpretation of Hegel, history begins with a "bloody battle" in which individuals demonstrate their humanity by risking their lives, a risk that is surrendered when they make the transition to a liberal society of mutual recognition. In liberal societies, conscription has been ended nearly everywhere, and genuine risk outsourced to specialists such as firefighters, emergency workers, and professional soldiers. There is no expectation that an ordinary citizen should risk his or her life for any cause. And that is the defect of liberalism: some people *want* to be able to risk "our Lives, our Fortunes and our sacred Honor" for a higher cause.

The intellectual godfather of this attitude was, as Strauss points out, Friedrich Nietzsche. What he and his nihilistic followers hated above all was the world of the "Last Man," the contented, unambitious, risk-averse creature who emerges at the end of history; that is, at the moment of the global victory of liberal democracy. Nietzsche attacked Christianity and its doctrine of the equal dignity of all human beings as the ultimate source of modern liberalism and democracy. He noted, however, that in his age Christianity no longer attracted belief: God had once lived, but now was dead.

The notion that the freedom enjoyed by people in a liberal society could be construed as aimlessness and triviality has many precursors. Socrates in Book VIII of *The Republic* has his own version of the Last Man in his description of a person living in a democracy:

> "Then," I said, "he also lives along day by day, gratifying the desire that occurs to him, at one time drinking and listening to the flute, at another downing water and reducing, now practicing gymnastics, and again idling and neglecting everything; and sometimes spending his time as though he were occupied with philosophy. Often he engages in politics and, jumping up, says and does whatever chances to come to him, and if he ever admires any soldiers, he turns in that direction, and if it's money-makers, in that one. And there is neither order nor necessity in his life, but calling this life sweet, free, and blessed he follows it throughout." (561c–d)

Strauss describes the attitude of the young Germans of his day as nihilistic, not because they were anarchists, but because their critique of modern liberalism did not yield a coherent vision of what would replace the existing consensus. In the Germany that Strauss had just fled, this led many to National Socialism. Nietzsche's relationship to the Nazis was complicated, but his ideas paved the way for their rise. For if God is dead and the religion that elevates slaves to be the equals of their masters is discredited, why not sign up with the doctrine that unapologetically promises to make you and your friends masters?

Strauss's 1941 lecture prefigures the current moment in eerie ways. Today's "post-liberals" do not have a coherent vision of what should replace liberalism. Some, such as Patrick Deneen and Adrian Vermeule, seem to hope for some form of Catholic integralism where society would agree on a set of strong moral principles defined by religion. Others, such as Curtis Yarvin and Costin Vlad Alamariu (aka "Bronze Age Pervert"), discard religion and long for a return of hierarchy and strong government. They are joined by some Silicon Valley moguls who believe that smarter and more successful people like themselves have a greater title to rule. What they all have in common is a hatred of a form of liberalism that forces everyone to declare their pronouns at the ends of emails to show the world that they are respectful of transgender people.

The absence of plausible visions for a better future society means that politicians and activists have to whip people into a panic over how bad the present is. What is striking about the protests, anger, and critiques of the liberal status quo in the America of the 2020s is how disproportionate they are to the lived reality of the protestors. This is nowhere more true than on the MAGA right. According to Donald Trump and many of his acolytes, the very existence of the United States is at stake; if the liberal candidate wins, "you won't have a country anymore." According to Michael Anton, the 2016 election was the last opportunity for passengers to rush the cockpit of the airplane before it crashed into the Capitol. According to Tim

Alberta's 2023 book on the evangelical right, many Christian nationalists believe that Christianity itself faces the threat of extinction and that liberals want to close down their churches. And many conservatives agree with the notion that we are living under a woke tyranny, in which it is impossible to dissent on a host of issues related to race, gender, sexual orientation, environment, and the like. They say this despite the fact that they themselves are expressing strong criticism of these very trends, and have elected a president who vows to reverse them.

Nor is it the case that economic desperation is the primary driver of right-wing rebellion. While working-class whites who lost their jobs to outsourcing may have been part of the original Trump coalition, the vast majority of protestors who turned up at the Capitol on January 6 were middle-class people with decent jobs. They showed up on that day because they believed in a concocted narrative about how the 2020 election had been stolen from them. They could play-act at being armed revolutionaries bravely defending their way of life, when the reality was that they were simply dupes enlisted to soothe the ego of a single narcissistic fraudster.

There has been growing economic inequality over the past two generations, with working-class incomes stagnating and a class of oligarchs pulling away from the rest of society. But the lived inequality today in the United States and other rich democracies such as in Europe is an inequality of respect. If people were simply demanding more resources, they would vote for social democratic politicians seeking to redistribute resources or offer more social protections. But the Left has been in retreat over the past two decades, with voters rejecting extensions of welfare-state benefits even if they materially benefit from them. What they want instead is respect.

The desire to struggle for the sake of struggle is evident as well on the left. The students who have set up pro-Palestinian encampments after October 7, 2023, on campuses across the United States are for the most part highly comfortable, privileged elites, going to top schools such as Harvard, Columbia, or UCLA. What they want is a break from their lives of steady but unheroic striving to get into those universities, and to experience danger and risk in pursuit of a just cause that has never previously been a major part of their lives. No more than the MAGA right do they have a clear vision of what type of future society they want to live in. This is not to deny the plight of Palestinian civilians trapped in Gaza, but these students are not similarly outraged at the situation of Ukrainians besieged by Russia or of victims of the civil war in Sudan.

There is no clear, systematic vision on the left for what kind of society should replace liberal democracy, as there once was. Many young people today have become, according to poll data, more sympathetic to socialism or Communism than previously. They are full of passion for social justice in terms of compensating specific identity groups for past wrongs, and they are full of hostility to "late-stage capitalism." But virtually all progressive visions for an alternative to current liberal order have been tried already. The extreme version of egalitarian justice that animated many leftists in the twentieth century, Marxism-Leninism, has been exposed as a moral atrocity after the collapse of Communism. Recent attempts to create this version of social justice have turned into nightmares, like the "twenty-first century socialism" of Hugo Chávez and Nicolás Maduro in Venezuela. The more moderate vision of social democracy has also been tried; indeed, many of its policies have already been happily incorporated into present-day social democratic welfare states. Some extreme environmentalists look to a future of "de-growth" to deal with the climate crisis, but honestly, who is going to risk their lives to get to a world where everyone gets poorer year after year? We are left with a small-bore agenda consisting of policies such as taxing billionaires, free bus rides and higher education, and so on. All of this does not constitute an attractive vision for a future world that is worth dying for.

There was a time when liberal democracy seemed like an exciting new idea, as it pushed aside earlier social orders based on tradition, inherited status, and fixed hierarchy. Meritocracy was not seen as a form of systemic racism; rather, it was a way for outsiders to break into circles of elite privilege. And indeed, liberal democracy is still inspiring to huge numbers of people around the world. Every year, tens if not hundreds of thousands undertake dangerous and expensive journeys from their homes in poor, unstable, violence-prone societies for the privilege of living in North America or Europe. Back at the time when I wrote "The End of History?" there was great excitement on the part of people in former Communist countries that they too would be able to experience the prosperity and personal freedom of life in a liberal democracy, as part of "Europe."

More than thirty-five years have passed since the fall of the Berlin Wall, and more than an entire generation has grown up in Eastern Europe since then with no direct experience of Communism or dictatorship. The European Union has fully delivered on its promise of peace and prosperity, yet many Europeans have come to see the EU itself as a tyranny. People in North America have had an even longer experience of stability, and are able to take the liberal democratic institutions that have produced that outcome for granted.

Of course, there is a lot that still needs to be accomplished. Racial justice remains elusive for many African Americans, there is a hugely inadequate response to the climate crisis, and wealth disparities remain enormous. But fixing these problems requires not radical change but the slow, steady work of reform: mobilizing, persuading, legislating, implementing policies, and building things, whether institutions or physical structures. A focus on real reform is *boring*: problems need to be fixed piecemeal and over long periods of time. No alternative social system that anyone has dreamed of to date will make them go away, nor will any charismatic leader break through today's constraints, despite promises that "I alone can fix it."

Democratic backsliding today is driven by activists who do not want to be "Last Men" tinkering with the house that has been built for them at the end of history. The problem, of course, is that struggling against liberal democracy is very likely to produce a worse world than the one we currently live in. That is the situation we face today, an outcome that was perfectly predictable more than thirty years ago.

Megalothymia is also playing out at a geopolitical level, where it is potentially much more dangerous. Both Russia and China are wounded great powers who feel that the US-dominated liberal world order of the last several decades does not grant them the status they deserve. Vladimir Putin has made very clear that he wants Russia to reclaim the superpower status it once enjoyed when it was part of the USSR. His ambitions include restoring the territorial extent of the former Soviet Union, dominating those countries surrounding it, and being consulted on every major global decision. China similarly speaks of the "one hundred years of humiliation" that it suffered from the Opium Wars in the nineteenth century until the formation of the People's Republic of China in 1949. It wants to be recognized as the guardian of a new world order fitting its own values and priorities.

What kind of a world order are we entering into in the third decade of the twenty-first century? It clearly doesn't fit neat ideological categories of the sort that characterized the Cold War and indeed much of the twentieth century. There is a broad cleavage between authoritarian countries and liberal democracies, but that cleavage doesn't explain the differences that exist within established democracies between elites and populists. What is particularly confusing about the present-day world is that populists within democracies are aligning themselves with external authoritarian partners. Thus Viktor Orbán's Fidesz, the Alternative for Germany, and the MAGA wing of the Republican Party have all found common cause with Putin's Russia on any number of issues. China has been invited into Europe, not because there is particular admiration for the China model, but because it is a way of thumbing one's nose at existing elites.

The current world order is divided, instead, by a cleavage between the humiliated and their former humiliators. There is huge resentment and anger against those elites who set the norms, standards, and expectations for behavior in previous years, and a desire to replace their world with a different one. But because we are indeed at the end of history, there is no clear vision for the sort of world that will replace the status quo.

We have means of distributing resources a bit more evenly, and should undertake to do that. What we lack is a way of distributing respect.

AFTERWORD: THE FUTURE OF LIBERAL DEMOCRACY

THERE HAS BEEN INCREASING EVIDENCE OF AND CONcern about democratic backsliding around the world. Most of the writing on this subject, to which I have myself contributed, is based on simple observation of global trends. Freedom House has documented declines in aggregate democracy scores for close to two decades now. The leading indicators of this decline include the rise of authoritarian great powers such as China and Russia; illiberal populist movements appearing in well-established democracies, including the United States; and the reemergence of interstate war and return of geopolitics—that is, rivalry, competition, and conflict among large nations.

All of these real-world developments are troubling, and could be precursors of even worse strife to come. These futures are intrinsically unknowable, and I don't want to speculate on what will happen in any particular country or region. When Alexandre Kojève taught his famous seminar on Hegel in the late 1930s and declared that history had ended in 1806, Europe was on the eve of a cataclysmic war, which gave way to a decades-long Cold War thereafter. This did not shake Kojève's belief in the essential correctness of the Hegelian story, since, as he explained, progress in history is neither uniform nor linear. For him, none of the perturbations of the nineteenth and twentieth centuries served to undermine the truth of the principles of the equality of freedom first articulated in the French Revolution.

Perhaps more important than an empirical analysis of contemporary political and geopolitical trends is a deeper investigation of those first principles themselves, and whether they are correct, coherent, and sustainable. To take a leaf from my own *Political Order* series, what drove historical progress was a long-term competition between alternative forms of political order, and the ability of their institutions to solve the internal and external challenges posed by their environment—physical, social, and technological. Thus hunter-gatherer bands could not compete with tribally organized societies, which in turn succumbed to state-level societies, especially after the invention of firearms eroded the power of mounted nomads. State-level societies developed increasingly complex institutions, which were better suited to managing the increasing social diversity of the societies over which they ruled.

Out of this evolutionary process was born modern liberal democracy. A liberal democracy balances three separate sets of institutions: a modern state, a rule of law, and institutions of democratic accountability. The first of these generates political power, which is necessary to protect the community from external and internal threats; the second and third constitute constraints on that power to make sure it is used for purposes serving community interests, and not just the interests of those individuals in control of the state. This balancing of power and constraint of power is one of the key challenges for a liberal democracy.

The world's political systems can be located on a spectrum of different balance points. A state that has neither rule of law nor democratic accountability is a dictatorship (China); a state with at least some semblance of rule of law but no electoral accountability is a liberal autocracy (Singapore or the UAE); a state with democratic accountability but a weak rule of law is an illiberal democracy (Hungary); and a weak state with some degree of rule of law and electoral accountability might be labeled an emerging democracy (this category is represented by a large number of countries in Latin America, sub-Saharan Africa, and other parts of the developing world). There are actually finer subcategories that emerge when we distinguish between patrimonial and modern states. As I argued in *Political Order and Political Decay*, there is constant pressure in modern states to move toward "repatrimonialization"; that is, regression of an impersonal, high-capacity state to one based on clientelism and patronage, often revolving around the friends and family of the ruler.

Any political system can be afflicted by insuperable external shocks (e.g., war, financial crisis, epidemics), and they can suffer from bad leaders and bad policy choices (e.g., inflationary policies, fiscal deficits, internal social conflicts based on class or ethnicity). These are "normal" challenges in the sense that they are not intrinsically rooted in the society's institutions. Mistakes in policy can be reversed by different policies; bad or incompetent leaders can be replaced by better leaders. One of the general arguments in favor of liberal democracies is that they have mechanisms for recovering from policy mistakes and can change leaders more readily than autocracies.

If we look to intrinsic challenges rooted in the theory and practice of liberal democracy, I would point to three that draw on some of the ideas I've covered earlier.

The first that is clearly intrinsic to liberalism has to do with what has been called the "fetish of proceduralism." To understand why this is a problem, we need to go back to my prior discussion of the need for delegation.

In early kinship-based societies, there are no formal procedures. Authority flows from the leader, whether a tribal chief or a big man. That individual is constrained by informal rules handed down in the form of custom. But as a society grows in scale, and particularly when state-level societies emerge, two things happen. First, the leader needs to delegate authority down a chain of command, leading to a fragmentation of authority. Second, informal rules tend to be replaced by formal ones. Informal rules have the great advantage of being adaptable to changing circumstances. But they are both less precise and easier to disregard or disobey. When a leader delegates authority to a hierarchy, there is a strong imperative to control that hierarchy through a system of formal rules.

Historically, the transition from informal customary rules to formal law occurred in many societies via organized religion. This was true in Christian Europe, early Islamic states, ancient Israel, Brahmin India, and China. Religious belief in a transcendental authority offered a great advantage in terms of enforcement: if you broke a law, the state might not be able to come after you or even notice your infraction, but you would be visible to a transcendental god or spirit that had great powers in the afterlife, if not in this one.

The establishment of formal law was thus initially a mechanism for controlling hierarchies. Law enabled the ruler to monitor and supervise the behavior of subordinates to whom he or she had delegated power, as well as ordinary people who might want to behave in unauthorized ways. This is what is known as "rule *by* law," where law simply reflects the will of the ruler.

In several societies, however, law came to be detached from the will of the ruler, and existed in a parallel hierarchy whose authority could rival that of the executive. This division of powers came to be known as "rule *of* law," where the ruler himself was expected to abide by a law that he or sometimes she did not completely control. Again, rule of law historically had religious roots, in the division between pope and emperor, sheikh and caliph, Brahmin and Kshatriya. This separation of law from executive authority reflected a certain social wisdom, that the ruler himself could become a tyrant and act against the interests of the people as a whole. Law by this understanding became the first "check and balance" constraining the will of the executive.

Law is not the only method of constraining executive authority. In Plato's *Republic*, the just city that Socrates constructs in speech does not envision anything like an independent judiciary as a check on power. Rather, he points to the moral education of rulers as a route to moderate government. Education of rulers was also a central part of Chinese culture. In early China, there was a prolonged debate between Legalists, such as Han Fei, and the Confucians. The

Legalists wanted to control society through comprehensive rule by law, in which the state enforced formal law by meting out harsh penalties. The Confucians, by contrast, argued that no set of formal rules could be adequate when applied in complex real-world situations. What was needed instead was a sage or wise ruler who could take context into account and arrive at suitably nuanced decisions.

The system that subsequently developed in dynastic China combined the two approaches. There was strict rule by law to control society, but also an elaborate set of institutions created to educate leaders on the basis of intellectual merit. It was China that invented meritocracy, many centuries before this became an established practice in the West. A poor boy from a backward province could take the exam for entrance into the mandarinate and potentially rise to become one of the most powerful men in the country. The social prestige of education remains strong in every East Asian society touched by Confucianism, and explains why Asian students tend to do well in schools across the United States and the rest of the West. The Chinese preference for education over law has led to a political system with few formal checks on power, but with a strong emphasis on educating a ruling class that would have wide discretionary authority to make decisions. This was true in dynastic China, and remains the case today in the contemporary PRC.

The West followed a different path, depending on formal law rather than education to limit state authority. There was good reason for this. Beginning in the early modern period, rule of law came to be seen as increasingly important to economic growth. One of the rights that law protected was the right of private property and to freedom of commerce. States and their rulers were typically predatory, and law existed to limit that predation. Since states did in fact need resources to fund their provision of public goods, arbitrary predation gradually evolved into taxation, which if held to a reasonable level could both fund things such as armies and security, and also permit citizens to enjoy the fruits of their labor.

As time went on, law proliferated and evolved at the highest level into constitutional systems that established multiple checks and balances to constrain executive authority. But formal law ramified downward as well, providing organizational principles governing corporations, labor unions, nongovernmental organizations, and the many social groups that make up modern societies.

Rule of law came to be venerated as one of the defining characteristics of Western civilization. Such veneration is a necessary condition for law's success, since most laws cannot be coercively enforced but depend on the normative adherence of individuals. But no rule-of-law society can do away with discretionary authority altogether. The Confucian admonition that no set of detailed laws can anticipate every possible future state of the world remains even more true today than in early China, as economies become more complex. Power needs to be delegated to lower levels of authority—levels that have local knowledge and the expertise necessary to act on such knowledge—rather than be controlled through ex ante rules.

"Procedural fetishism" occurs when political actors come to regard procedures and rules as ends in themselves, as opposed to mechanisms for achieving the collective purposes of government. This is particularly true in the United States, where distrust of government is a foundation of political culture, and law is seen as a primary means of controlling power. But it is a problem in other Western liberal democracies as well. Bureaucratic dysfunction is rampant in the United States and Europe, where governing authorities have bound themselves with endless layers of detailed rules, like the Federal Acquisition Regulations that regulate procurement in America, or the *acquis communautaire* developed by the European Union. In the United States, governors find they cannot do things such as rebuild critical highways without violating multiple rules, and need to find workarounds to in effect suspend the rule of law. In Latin America, procedural rules have made it difficult to apprehend and convict gang members and narco-traffickers, who take advantage of legal systems to avoid accountability for their crimes.

Procedural fetishism then paves the way for its opposite: wholesale abandonment of the rule of law by authoritarian rulers. The democratic backsliding that we have seen since the early 2000s is in the first instance a retreat less from democracy than from the rule of law. Citizens unhappy about the slowness or inability of democratic governments to deal with issues such as crime or migration have voted for populist politicians and strongman rulers who promise to cut through the red tape and get things done. They dream about vigilantes who can punish criminals quickly and efficiently, without all the legal procedures that existing police and prosecutors have to follow. One of the great appeals of China is its manifest ability to build things more quickly and at a lower cost than rule-bound Western competitors.

Authoritarian governments face few procedural checks on their power. As a result, they can do amazing things. Dictatorial power allowed Deng Xiaoping to make big decisions rapidly, such as the dismantling of central planning in China and the creation of a market economy. By liberalizing the system inherited from Mao Zedong, Deng benefited Chinese society in incalculable ways. But the same unconstrained system enabled him to implement the "one child" policy that allowed the state to interfere with personal life on a massive scale, and earlier permitted Mao himself to launch disastrous policies, such as the Great Leap Forward and the Cultural Revolution. The current leader, Xi Jinping, has relaxed the few rules that existed under Deng, such as term limits for senior leaders, and has already made big policy mistakes, such as zero-Covid, that would have been avoided by the earlier post-Deng system of collective leadership.

Proceduralism is driven by fundamental commitments embraced by liberalism itself. Liberals understand the rule of law to be in the first instance a means of protecting the dignity and rights of all individuals from the power of the state. The great victories of liberalism during the Civil Rights era in the United States revolved around extending rights and legal protections to African Americans, who were among the most marginalized of all Americans. These legal protections were then applied to an expanding range of groups, including women, gays and lesbians, consumers, small businesses, religious minorities, transgender people, the disabled, immigrants, and even corporations making political donations. Social objectives such as worker safety and environmental protection were understood by many liberals to be basic rights rather than interests, which had two deleterious effects. If something is understood to be a basic right, it is hard to argue for trading it off against some other social good, such as economic growth or effective government. Second, rights need to be adjudicated in the courts rather than reconciled by legislatures or bureaucracies. There is a tendency, visible today in conservative American jurisprudence, to draw every issue into the legal system, which is often the least efficient way of resolving knotty social conflicts. But this is also true in many other liberal democracies, where newer constitutions have embedded social policies into hard law as second-generation rights. Here as well, courts lack the authority or capacity to make what are essentially difficult political decisions, turning citizens against the courts and rule of law as such. Rolling back proceduralism in the interest of delivering effective government in a more measured way has not been accomplished in many contemporary liberal democracies.

So this is the first intrinsic problem with liberal societies. They seem to be doomed to create governments of increasing size and complexity, with millions of lines of laws and regulations that even big data technologies have trouble keeping up with. In principle, they could reverse this process and greatly simplify their codes, but none have made much progress in this direction. They have a very difficult time finding a middle ground between paralyzing proceduralism and overt authoritarian government.

The second question haunting liberalism has to do with whether there are intrinsic limits to moral freedom. Liberalism is a doctrine that protects an individual's right to choose, which is regarded as the source of equal human dignity. That right has always been understood to be limited in certain ways: individuals don't have the right to deprive other individuals of their rights, and in general must accommodate themselves to the requirements of living with other rights-bearers in society. Over time, our idea of moral autonomy has expanded well beyond inherited moral systems, such as those dictated by the world's traditional religions. Individuals can make up their own social rules, the only limitation typically being physical harm to others (e.g., no religions involving human sacrifice).

There have always been two divergent interpretations of liberalism. As noted in an earlier chapter, the tradition beginning with Thomas Hobbes, John Locke, and Jean-Jacques Rousseau starts with substantive accounts of human nature, and they derive political rights from those understandings. Hobbes and Rousseau may disagree about the nature of human nature (e.g., whether humans are intrinsically violent and selfish, or isolated and peaceful), but they both derive the human "ought" from the human "is."

There is an alternative approach to liberalism, however, that begins with Immanuel Kant and continues through modern Kantians such as John Rawls. This strand eschews a substantive theory of human nature and reduces human uniqueness to the capacity for choice. From this premise, both Kant and Rawls derive categorical rules that would apply to rational creatures regardless of their intrinsic natures. In Kant's words, they would apply equally to a "society of devils." This understanding maximizes individual choice, often at the expense of human community.

Actual liberal societies retain many assumptions about human nature and the intrinsic desirability of particular behaviors. Legal systems continue to calibrate punishments based on understandings of the moral seriousness of various crimes, which in turn reflects assumptions about how typical human beings are expected to behave. We create rights to freedom of speech, belief, and association because we feel these faculties are critical to human life.

What we might call the Kantian or Rawlsian strand of liberalism prioritizes individual choice or autonomy over social goods. Does the moral freedom protected by liberalism include the right to choose not just our behavior but our natures as well? In the not-too-distant future, technological advances will provide an even greater range of interventions that will allow us to change our natures, and those of our descendants as well.

Is there a core set of human attributes that we believe qualifies an individual to be called a human being, with all of the rights and protections that such status confers in liberal societies? In *Our Posthuman Future*, I referred to a "Factor X," a set of characteristics that were hard to define precisely but were nonetheless highly meaningful to most people. A lot of what I thought filled Factor X had to do with our consciousness and emotions, particularly those having to do with our social proclivities: our ability to feel pain, love, anger, sympathy, and pity. Even though animals can share certain human characteristics, most people do not believe that they qualify for the full set of rights that a human does, because they do not possess the whole of Factor X. Similarly, a sociopath is someone who does not feel emotions such as compassion and pity, and every society in the world feels entitled to limit their basic rights, including, in extreme cases, their right to life.

The fundamental problem with this Kantian-Rawlsian understanding of liberalism is its tendency to strip human beings down to the capacity for choice. The dominant concern for this type of liberal is protection of that single, nonconformist voice. But human nature—Factor X—is much more capacious than that mere autonomy; people also want a sense of community, which is based on an underlying feeling of shared humanity. *Thymos* here is critical, because it is the part of the soul that demands recognition by other people. Pace Rousseau, we are not isolated individuals who can thrive in the absence of the approbation of other people. We recognize the sufferings, labors, anxieties, hopes, struggles, and achievements of others to the extent that we have experienced them ourselves. But is community possible with beings who lack some important part of Factor X, who in particular lack *thymos*? How would we feel about beings who have deliberately placed themselves outside of that shared experience? Would we admire an athlete who constantly broke speed records because they were artificially enhanced? We already discount the achievements of those who use performance-enhancing drugs. And what about a math genius whose powers were assisted by an implanted chip? Would we want biomedical technology to make our children more compliant with social rules?

From a different direction, artificial intelligence may generate claims that a machine possesses Factor X, and therefore is entitled to the protection of its rights. There are many people in the tech world who believe that the human brain is simply a "wet computer," and that when computers reach the scale of human brains they will also develop human attributes such as consciousness and the ability to feel emotions. With the advent of generative AI, we are a bit closer to that goal. Since we don't have a theory of what Factor X is or where it comes from, such arguments will be appealing to many and may become the grounds for machines to claim political rights. But will we really feel solidarity in a community made up of humans and quasi humans?

These kinds of considerations speak to liberalism's intrinsic problem with diversity. As I noted in *Liberalism and Its Discontents*, liberalism as a doctrine arose initially in the seventeenth century as a means of *managing* diversity. The problematic form of diversity back then was religious, as Protestants and Catholics spent decades fighting one another for political supremacy. Liberalism managed diversity by lowering the aspirations of politics: the state got out of the business of dictating final ends as defined by religion; individuals were free to practice their faith, but needed to tolerate people with other views and practices.

Diversity can be a good thing in terms of fostering creativity and innovation. But it's not necessarily a good thing in and of itself. Liberal societies tolerate diversity, but only within certain bounds. There has to be general consensus within liberal societies on liberal rules of the road. As I argued at some length in *Liberalism and Its Discontents*, liberal societies need national identities, ideally identities built around the idea of liberalism itself. In the United States, that would mean loyalty to the US Constitution and Declaration of Independence. In Germany, Jürgen Habermas has spoken of a *Verfassungspatriotismus*, or "constitutional patriotism," to unite an increasingly diverse German society.

The problem is that such civic identities are necessarily thin, given the de facto cultural diversity of modern liberal societies. Older national identities have been built around shared history, language, culture, religion, food, holidays, and indeed race and ethnicity. And yes, such identities exert a much stronger emotional pull when you share those common characteristics. Much of the appeal of right-wing politics today lies in the narrower but stronger sense of community such movements offer, from Narendra Modi's Hindutva to

Christian nationalists in the United States. The central challenge for contemporary liberals is how to thicken our sense of national identity without veering off in an overtly illiberal direction.

The desire for community based on what R. R. Reno labels "strong gods" can be wholly satisfied in liberal societies through a dense civil society in which people are drawn together by shared passions and interests. Churches and other groups of religious believers, ethnically and racially based affinity groups, and groups defined by gender or sexual orientation all have a right to exist and indeed are very powerful in modern liberal societies. The only condition that liberalism imposes is tolerance for a pluralism of communities organized around differing beliefs.

The particular challenge for a liberal national identity at present is that with the rise of the internet, many groups in civil society have moved online, where they are no longer constrained by geographical propinquity or by the rules of civility that human beings have evolved to moderate face-to-face interactions. The self-interest of the large tech platforms that host social media networks encourages extremism among online communities, since this generates more engagement. The internet has undermined many of the older institutions that filtered and mediated information. The online world in which many people now live and interact can be wholly detached from reality, and malevolent actors can make use of the enormous reach of social media to generate alternative realities. The result is a highly polarized and fragmented society, where the civic virtues needed to sustain a liberal democracy are eroded.

The final issue that haunts liberalism and liberal democracy is the one that constitutes the title of this book. Liberalism by its very success breeds peaceful, prosperous societies that seem to flatten human horizons. Such societies may be better than the dictatorships, theocracies, and aggressive nationalisms out of which they arose, but people's memories are punctuated in generational cycles, and their expectations for politics keep expanding faster than the rate at which political institutions can change. People will want to continue to struggle for just causes, even if they cannot fully articulate what a fully just society would look like.

No one to date has come up with a novel architecture to house the Last Man at the end of history, but that aspiration inevitably remains.

ANNOTATED BIBLIOGRAPHY

In place of a conventional bibliography, I am providing a reader's guide to the books and articles that have shaped my thinking over several decades, particularly on the subject of hierarchies and delegation. I've included a couple of my own academic articles on issues of governance that may have escaped the attention of general readers.

Bagley, Nicholas. "The Procedure Fetish," *Michigan Law Review* 118 (2019): 345–401. This article points to the tendency of liberals (and liberal societies) to seek legitimacy through the multiplication of procedural rules, in ways that prevent them from using government power to accomplish the ends they seek.

Banfield, Edward C. *The Moral Basis of a Backward Society.* Free Press (1958). This ethnographic study of a small town in Southern Italy was written after Banfield had completed a similar study of a Mormon town in Utah. He saw an enormous difference in the degree of social relatedness in the two places, and invented the term "amoral familism" to describe the lack of what was later called social capital in Southern Italy. Robert Putnam later confirmed many of Banfield's observations empirically in his book *Making Democracy Work: Civic Traditions in Modern Italy.*

Carpenter, Daniel P. *The Forging of Bureaucratic Autonomy: Reputations, Networks, and Policy Innovation in Executive Agencies, 1862–1928.* Princeton University Press (2001). Carpenter provides a historical account of the rise of two of the earliest federal agencies, the

US Department of Agriculture and the US Postal Service. As they broke away from the corruption of the patronage system after the Pendleton Act, their effectiveness was enhanced by their autonomy from democratic politics.

Chandler, Alfred D. *The Visible Hand: The Managerial Revolution in American Business*. Harvard University Press (1977). I read this book while writing *Trust*, which traces the historical evolution of the modern corporate form of organization in the United States. One of the big issues is how societies make the transition from family businesses to large, impersonal organizations, and Chandler provides insight into this topic.

Coase, Ronald H. "The Nature of the Firm." *Economica* 6 (1937): 386–405. It took this paper for the field of economics to recognize the importance of hierarchies. Ronald Coase was an economist at the University of Chicago who asked why hierarchies existed given that conventional economic theory argued that decentralized markets were optimal ways of allocating resources. The reason for the existence of huge corporations was, he argued, transaction costs that made centralized decision-making more efficient.

Coase, Ronald H. "The Problem of Social Cost." *Journal of Law and Economics* 3 (1960): 1–44. This article addresses the problem of farmers and ranchers, the latter of whose cattle would often invade and spoil the farmers' lands. Coase noted that the farmers and ranchers could get to a fair distribution by negotiating with one another if their property rights were well specified, and if transaction costs were low.

DiIulio, John J. Jr. "Principled Agents: The Cultural Bases of Behavior in a Federal Government Bureaucracy." *Journal of Public Administration Research and Theory* 4 (1994): 277–320. A lot of economic theorizing about hierarchies took the form of principal-agent models, in which dysfunctions such as corruption occurred when agents followed their own interests rather than carrying out the mandates of their principals. Economists tended to think in terms of incentive alignment, but DiIulio argues that agents were often directed not by material rewards but by internalized norms guiding proper behavior.

Dunkelman, Marc. *Why Nothing Works: Who Killed Progressivism and How to Bring it Back*. Public Affairs (2025). This book traces the history of what the author calls the Hamiltonian and Jeffersonian strands of progressive thinking in the United States. The former sees the government as an instrument of progressive reform; the latter fears the government and seeks to check centralized power by spreading it out to as many other parts of society as possible. The country swung toward Jeffersonianism during the 1960s, leading to the present problem of "vetocracy."

Evans, Peter B. *Embedded Autonomy: States and Industrial Transformation*. Princeton University Press (1995). Evans was one of the first political scientists to point to bureaucratic autonomy as one of the conditions for the successful development of East Asian societies such as Japan and Korea. These countries devolved authority to technocrats, but ensured that they were still responsive to societal needs. This kind of autonomy did not exist in other parts of the developing world such as Latin America or the Middle East.

Fischer, David Hackett. *Albion's Seed: Four British Folkways in America*. Oxford University Press (1991). This book explains much of American history in terms of the interactions of four specific English settler groups: the Puritans, descendants of the royalist Cavaliers from the English Civil War, the Quakers, and the "Scotch-Irish." The American Civil War could in many ways be understood as a conflict between the first two of these communities, and populism from Andrew Jackson to the present, as well as the American gun culture, as a legacy of the Scotch-Irish. The historical analysis is truly revelatory.

Fukuyama, Francis. "What Is Governance?" *Governance* 26 (2013): 347–68. This is my one claim to being a public administration theorist. I point to the importance of bureaucratic autonomy to the proper functioning of an administrative hierarchy. But what determines how much authority should be delegated to lower levels of the organization? I suggest that the proper degree would depend on the capacity of the agents. In a high-capacity organization such as a central bank or finance ministry, a high degree of autonomy is appropriate, while in a low-capacity organization such as a customs agency, administrative discretion should be minimized.

Fukuyama, Francis, and Katherine Bersch. "Defining Bureaucratic Autonomy." *Annual Review of Political Science* 26 (2023): 213–32. It is a common trope on the right to argue that "unelected bureaucrats" have escaped the control of democratically elected politicians and implemented their own left-wing agenda. This article explores the way that the federal bureaucracy remains firmly under the control of elected officials, who for reasons of their own choose not to exercise the controls and oversight available to them.

Fustel de Coulanges, Numa Denis. *The Ancient City*. Doubleday Anchor Books (1965). This book is a revelation regarding Greek and Roman religion before the rise of the Olympian gods. Fustel de

Coulanges traces a form of ancestor worship to ancient Aryan customs that regarded the spirits of dead ancestors as inhabiting the ground where they were buried, and who had to be appeased by their descendants with gifts of food and drink. These beliefs are characteristic of many other societies organized into segmentary lineages; going beyond Fustel de Coulanges, they explain similar behaviors from the Mexican Day of the Dead to the tomb-sweeping ceremonies in Taiwan.

Gambetta, Diego. *The Sicilian Mafia: The Business of Private Protection.* Harvard University Press (1993). This book provides a convincing economic explanation for the rise of the Mafia in Sicily. That explanation revolves around the weakness of the nineteenth-century state, which could not guarantee property rights adequately. Individuals were forced to turn to private protection, which is the origin of the Mafioso, or "man of honor." Something similar has happened in Mexico, Colombia, and other countries with weak states, where local mafias were enlisted to protect property rights and morphed into criminal organizations making use of private enforcement power.

Gellner, Ernest. *Nations and Nationalism.* Second edition. Cornell University Press (2006). Gellner, a social anthropologist, developed a theory of nationalism that linked it to the needs of an industrial society. The demand for a common language reflected the needs of a workplace in which diverse people needed to cooperate, and explained why nationalism first appeared in the wake of the French Revolution.

Haidt, Jonathan. *The Righteous Mind: Why Good People Are Divided by Politics and Religion.* Pantheon (2012). In this book Haidt explains how human rationality often takes the form of "motivated reasoning," in which people marshal facts to support favored conclusions, rather than deriving conclusions from facts. It explains many of the contradictions of our present-day politics.

Hayek, Friedrich A. "The Use of Knowledge in Society." *American Economic Review* 35 (1945): 519–30. In the 1940s, Friedrich Hayek was engaged in a debate with Joseph Schumpeter on the relative merits of Communism and capitalism as economic systems. At the time of the debate, the answer wasn't obvious: Western capitalism was recovering from the Great Depression, while the Soviet Union was the world's fastest-growing economy in the 1930s. In this article, Hayek argues that the vast majority of information in a modern economy is local in nature, and that market economies could better respond to local information through decentralized bargaining between buyers and sellers. For me, this insight explains why hierarchical organizations need to delegate authority down to the lowest possible level, to take advantage of local knowledge and to be able to respond to information quickly.

Hirschman, Albert O. *Exit, Voice, and Loyalty: Responses to Decline in Firms, Organizations, and States*. Harvard University Press (1970). This short book (all of Hirschman's books were short) provides a conceptual basis for organizational and political reform. Members of a dysfunctional organization face a choice of either exiting the organization and allowing it to fail, or remaining as participants and trying to reform it from within. Hirschman is effectively in dialogue with Milton Friedman, who pushed for exit options out of the public sector such as vouchers and school choice. Hirschman demonstrates the limits of exit, and indicates where organizational loyalty might provide a better path to change.

Hirschman, Albert O. *Journeys Toward Progress: Studies of Economic Policy-Making in Latin America*. Twentieth Century Fund (1963). This book traces Colombia's efforts at land reform in the 1930s, and how they succeeded in making incremental progress on a question central to that country's stability as a democracy. Unfortunately those gains were reversed with the civil conflicts of the 1950s and the rise of the drug trade and the FARC in the 1970s. This is a problem still unresolved by that country.

Hirschman, Albert O. *The Passions and the Interests: Political Arguments for Capitalism Before Its Triumph*. Princeton University Press (1977). It is remarkable how Hirschman, a development economist, could use a sabbatical to read deeply into seventeenth- and eighteenth-century philosophy and social theory, and extract from that important insights into the moral transformation that was necessary to permit the flourishing of modern capitalism. Aristocratic societies prized honor above gain and placed limits on the accumulation of wealth; it was only with the rise of a bourgeois culture that modern market economies could flourish and spread.

Huntington, Samuel P. *Political Order in Changing Societies*. Yale University Press (1968). This was Sam Huntington's first and in many ways most important book. It undermined postwar modernization theory, which argued that all good things—economic growth, social transformation, democracy, stability, and law—went together in a seamless modernization process. This book shows how these different aspects of modernization could work at cross-purposes; for example, how economic growth could lead to modernization in ways that produce instability rather than order. He focuses the attention of political science on the question of order, which he argues needs to precede democracy.

Jacobs, Jane. *The Death and Life of Great American Cities.* Random House (1961). In this classic work of urbanology, Jane Jacobs, author and activist, explains how in cities with mixed-use neighborhoods, public safety was not maintained by a heavy police presence or surveillance; rather, it stemmed from the presence of adults in the neighborhood who could maintain a normative watch over the behavior of young people. This was what she called "social capital," which was lacking in the desolate urban towers that constituted public housing in the 1950s. She was the big opponent of builders such as New York City's Robert Moses, who took little account of the social life of the neighborhoods he bulldozed.

Klitgaard, Robert E. *Controlling Corruption.* University of California Press (1988). Klitgaard, a well-known expert on corruption, devised the formula Corruption = Monopoly + Discretion – Accountability. This seemed to me a conundrum, because many bureaucracies ran better when bureaucrats were given more discretion. Thinking this through led to my *Governance* article linking levels of discretion to state capacity.

Lilla, Mark. *The Reckless Mind: Intellectuals in Politics.* New York Review of Books Press (2016). Lilla analyzes the writings of a number of twentieth-century intellectuals who strayed into politics, including postmodernists Jacques Derrida and Michel Foucault, and explores the contradictions their thought entailed.

MacIntyre, Alasdair. *After Virtue.* University of Notre Dame Press (1981). MacIntyre was one of a group of "communitarian" critics of Rawlsian liberalism. Rawls's *Theory of Justice* emphasizes the need to protect individual autonomy and the need for each person to pursue their own vision of the good life. MacIntyre argues that such a society lacks any common understanding of virtue, without which any true human community could not exist. What is needed today is classical republicanism; that is, a liberalism that is built around a substantive view of virtue.

Maine, Henry. *Ancient Law: Its Connection with the Early History of Society and Its Relation to Modern Ideas.* Beacon Press (1963). Maine was an English legal theorist who spent many years in British India, and traced the origins of European law to its Aryan roots. This book puts forth the famous dichotomy between "status" and "contract" as a characteristic of modern societies. In the latter, labor was a commodity that could be freely bought and sold in labor markets, in contrast to premodern societies in which you were born into an occupation and social status over which you had no control.

Malone, Thomas, and Joanne Yates. "Electronic Markets and Electronic Hierarchies." *Communications of the ACM* 30 (1987): 484–97. In this article, Malone and Yates argue that if hierarchies are necessitated by transaction costs, as Coase's theory of the firm indicated, then the advent of the internet and rapid and cheap communications should reduce those transaction costs and make horizontal coordination much easier. They suggest that there is an intermediate space between markets and hierarchies consisting of electronically mediated networks.

North, Douglass C. *Institutions, Institutional Change, and Economic Performance.* Cambridge University Press (1990). Doug North, an economic historian, single-handedly brought the study of institutions into development economics with this book. Amazingly enough, economic growth models before this point did not make reference to politics or institutions; after North, they could not avoid the subject. Later institutional economists such as Daron Acemoglu owe a lot to his pioneering work.

Olson, Mancur. *The Logic of Collective Action: Public Goods and the Theory of Groups.* Harvard University Press (1965). This book, for which Olson would have won an economics Nobel Prize had he lived longer, established the basic theory of collective action that is still useful across the social sciences. He argues that as the scale of organizations grows, various forms of cheating and shirking become harder to detect, which then requires formal mechanisms (such as mandatory taxation) to control. Political power is based on who is the best organized, which in turn is the result of which groups can resolve their collective action problems most readily. (I got to know Olson, by the way, when we were both invited to a corporate event in Germany, and were stiffed of our speaking fees. We commiserated as our lawyers sought restitution for the two of us.)

Olson, Mancur. *The Rise and Decline of Nations.* Yale University Press (1982). This book in many ways explains the current predicament of the American economy, and why so many sectors from real estate to health care are dysfunctional. Olson argues that democracies tend to accumulate interest groups that proliferate over time and use their political power to protect the interests of established players. He suggests that the only way out of this is war, revolution, or a dramatic financial crisis that wipes out entrenched incumbents and allows the economy to start out all over again.

Pahlka, Jennifer. *Recoding America: Why Government Is Failing in the Digital Age and How We Can Do Better.* Metropolitan Books (2023). Jen Pahlka is a technologist who founded Code for America, an organization seeking to guide young technologists into government, and was one of the founders of the US Digital Service in the Obama administration. Her brilliant book is based on her personal experience in government, both in California and in Washington, the latter during the Healthcare.gov meltdown. She shows how it is the overregulation of bureaucrats that makes them so slow and inefficient, and how a truly effective government needs to liberate them to use their own common sense and judgment to solve problems.

Pippin, Robert B. "Being, Time, and Politics: The Strauss-Kojève Debate." *History and Theory* 32 (1993): 138–61. A useful introduction to this complex relationship.

Putnam, Robert D. *Making Democracy Work: Civic Traditions in Modern Italy.* Princeton University Press, 1993. Putnam here provides empirical backing for the widely recognized differences between Northern and Southern Italy, as earlier described by Edward Banfield's observations about "amoral familism."

Shulsky, Abram N., and Francis Fukuyama. *The Virtual Corporation and Army Organization.* Rand Corporation (1997). This Rand study opened my eyes to the importance of delegation in military organizations, and the way in which German *Auftragstaktik* had been incorporated into US military doctrine in the wake of the Vietnam War. It also taught me how important long-term career paths are as incentives, and how critical the HR function is to the functioning of organizations.

Simon, Herbert. *Public Administration.* Knopf (1961). This was for many years the standard book on public administration. Among its many insights, one thing stood out to me: Simon's observation that authority in hierarchical organizations often flows from the bottom to the top rather than the reverse direction, as principal-agent theory suggested. This is because low-level agents often have expertise and knowledge that their superiors lack, and constitutes another reason why delegation and bureaucratic autonomy are necessary.

Smith, Adam. *An Inquiry into the Nature and Causes of the Wealth of Nations.* Liberty Classics (1981). The *Wealth of Nations* is of course taken as a defense of capitalism by the latter's friends and foes alike. But for my money, the most important passages are those in the first three chapters that talk about the pin factory and use it to illustrate basic concepts such as economies of scale, the division of labor, and trade as the primary drivers of economic growth. Smith's celebration of the division of labor would be attacked by Karl Marx in *The Communist Manifesto*, and greatly expanded upon by Émile Durkheim.

Strauss, Leo. *Natural Right and History.* University of Chicago Press (1953). Most of Leo Strauss's books were dense interpretations of important thinkers such as Maimonides, Hobbes, Spinoza, and Machiavelli. This book presents a more linear account of the transition from ancients to moderns, including interpretations of individual thinkers, and draws out the connective links between them.

Taylor, Charles. *Sources of the Self: The Making of the Modern Identity.* Harvard University Press (1989). My own work owes a great deal to Charles Taylor. He writes at length about Hegel and the importance of recognition, and his book on the self is foundational to any study of modern identity politics. He chronicles the rise of the inner self as one of the characteristics of contemporary liberalism.

Tocqueville, Alexis de. *The Old Regime and the Revolution.* University of Chicago Press (1998). Less well-known than *Democracy in America*, this book came out of Tocqueville's study of manor records and *doléances* before the French Revolution. It is full of incredible insights, such as the dependence of the French on state intervention, and the notion that the French Revolution was triggered not by deteriorating conditions but by the fact that things were getting better, but not at a rate that kept up with rising expectations. It was introduced to Chinese readers by Wang Qishan, and convinced many people in the Chinese Communist Party not to start down the slippery slope of gradual reform as Gorbachev had done. I particularly admire the fact that Tocqueville did a huge amount of primary research for this book at a late point in his life, when many intellectuals would be resting on their laurels.

Waldrop, M. Mitchell. *Complexity: The Emerging Science at the Edge of Order and Chaos.* Simon and Schuster (1992). This is a good layperson's guide to the study of complex adaptive systems. The basic insight is that order often emerges not out of a top-down plan or hierarchy, but rather through the interaction of lower-level agents following simple rules. A flock of birds is not directed by a chief bird, but rather emerges through each individual bird following a relatively simple algorithm. To this day, complexity has never been formalized either as a theory or as a tool for analysis, but it is obviously very important.

Weber, Max. *From Max Weber: Essays in Sociology.* Oxford University Press (1946). This collection of Weber essays (which I inherited from my father) contains some of his most famous. "Politics as a

Vocation" presents Weber's widely used definition of the state as a legitimate monopoly of violence over territory, and speaks of politics as the "slow boring of hard boards" that requires both commitment and compromise. His essays on bureaucracy not only define the term but establish his categories of traditional, legal/rational, and charismatic authority, as well as articulate his observation about the "routinization of charisma." And his essay "The Protestant Sects and the Spirit of Capitalism," while not as famous as his book on Calvinism, notes how the sectarian nature of American Protestantism has encouraged what Tocqueville described as the "art of association."

Wilson, James Q. *Bureaucracy: What Government Agencies Do and Why They Do It.* Basic Books (1988). This edited volume constitutes a classic comparative study of bureaucracies across different societies, a topic that has been neglected by mainstream political science.

Womack, James P. *The Machine That Changed the World: The Story of Lean Production.* Harper Perennial (1991). This was one of many books published in the 1980s and 1990s that sought to explain Toyota's *kanban*, or just-in-time, system to readers in North America and Europe. Many outside observers saw just-in-time as a method for economizing on inventory costs. Womack explains how the system was really about quality control: empowering low-level factory-floor workers to call out problems allowed defects to be controlled before they were introduced into the production process. Western car companies, by contrast, tolerated the defects and hoped to correct them in rework areas at the end of the production line, something that never worked well.

ACKNOWLEDGMENTS

I AM VERY GRATEFUL TO MY TWO EDITORS, ERIC CHINSKI at Farrar, Straus and Giroux and Andrew Franklin at Profile Books, for having shepherded this manuscript to publication. Eric has edited the last five of my books, and Andrew all eleven. Their comments, as well as those of my longtime literary agent, Esther Newberg at Creative Artists Agency, were of course invaluable. These three, plus my wife, Laura, were the only ones to see the manuscript prior to its final version, and I am very grateful to Laura for her support over the years. I would also like to thank the teams at Farrar, Straus and Giroux, Creative Artists Agency, and Profile Books for their meticulous work. I should note that I was able to draw on the compilation of family documents by my late aunt, Fumiko Ide, and that letters from my Uncle Hiroo were provided by my German cousin Katharina Schaffer von Baibus. Fei Yan helped secure the rights to the photo of the Covid ward in China.

INDEX

Page numbers in *italics* refer to photos.